A TREATISE ON CHANCEL SCREENS AND ROOD LOFTS

A TREATISE ON CHANCEL SCREENS AND ROOD LOFTS

AUGUSTUS WELBY NORTHMORE PUGIN

ISBN: 978-93-93693-37-2

Published: 1851

LECTOR HOUSE LLP
E-MAIL: lectorpublishing@gmail.com

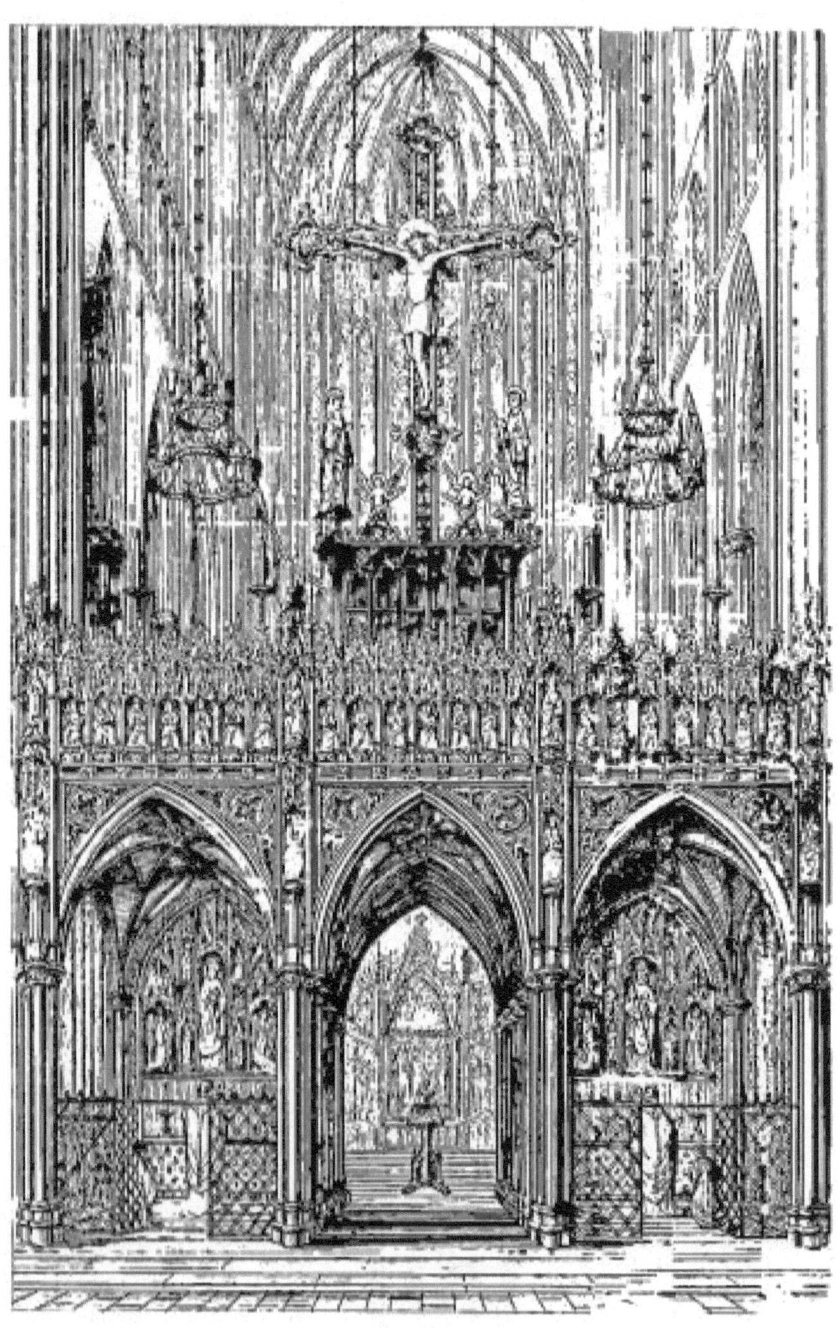

A Cathedral Screen.

A Parochial Screen.

A TREATISE ON CHANCEL SCREENS AND ROOD LOFTS,

THEIR ANTIQUITY, USE, AND SYMBOLIC SIGNIFICATION

BY

A. WELBY PUGIN, ARCHITECT

ILLUSTRATED WITH FIGURES COPIED ON STONE FROM DRAWINGS BY THE AUTHOR

NE TRANSGREDIARIS TERMINOS QUOS POSUERUNT PATRES TUI.

1851

CONTENTS

Page

LIST OF PLATES

A TREATISE ON ROOD SCREENS, &C.

INTRODUCTION.

THE subject on which I am about to treat is one of far more importance than the generality of men may be willing to admit; it is not a mere question of architectural detail, respecting a few mullions and a transverse beam, but it involves great principles connected with discipline, and even faith, and it is a question in which all those who either wish for the revival of ancient solemnity and reverence, or even the preservation of what yet remains, are most deeply interested. The contest that has been raised by the restoration of screens in England is not altogether new; it occurred in France during the latter part of the last century, when a vile spirit of modern innovation appears to have arisen among a portion of the French clergy, chiefly in the capitular bodies, and more injury was then inflicted on the great churches of that country than was caused by the outrages of the Calvinists and Huguenots in the civil wars of the sixteenth century. The traditions of the church, as regards the *disposition* and *arrangement* of ecclesiastical buildings in the northern countries, do not appear to have been much affected by the revived paganism of the sixteenth century; the details were debased and incongruous, but the *things* remained unaltered *in principle*,—rood lofts were erected, choirs were stalled, cruciform churches, with aisles and lateral and lady chapels, and transepts, were the general type followed,[1] and screens for choirs, side chapels, and altars were universal. But gradually, from the adoption of the details of classic antiquity, the buildings themselves became objects of imitation, till revived paganism displayed its full absurdity in the substitution of a temple of Jupiter for a church of the crucified Redeemer in the huge *room* called the Madeleine. Designed by infidels, built by infidels, and suited only for infidel purposes, and then turned over, for want of another use, to become a church!

The very decorations are an insult to Christianity; an ambitious conqueror, set up as a deity, occupying the place of our divine Redeemer himself, a mockery and a terrible blasphemy against that God to whose service the place has been

[1] The church of St. Eustache, Paris, is a striking example of a pointed church, both in plan, disposition, and proportion, carried out in Italian detail; but even much later, the churches of St. Roch and St. Sulpice, in the same city, were constructed on Catholic traditions, although all trace of the ancient detail has disappeared; they are *cruciform*, *choral*, and *absidal*, with *aisles* and chapels, a clerestory, and vaulting supported by flying buttresses, and the latter has even two great western towers for bells. Notwithstanding their debased detail, these edifices have still the character of churches, and are adapted by their *arrangement* for the celebration of Catholic rites.

unfortunately devoted; moreover, this monument of absurd impiety has been raised at a greater cost than what would have produced one of the fairest churches of mediæval construction, and it is so practically unsuited for even the ordinary requirements of a church, that there are no means for hanging bells, but a vain attempt was made of suspending them in the roof, where they stunned all *within* the building, and were inaudible to those *without*, for whose benefit they were intended, and, after a short trial, they were finally removed.

I have been induced to speak particularly of this edifice, as it is the beau ideal of a modern church in the minds of those who are opposed to screens; for the principles of these men, worked out to their legitimate ends, are subversive of every tradition and the whole system of ecclesiastical architecture. Screens are, in truth, the very least part of the cause of their animosity to the churches of their Fathers, for if any man says he loves pointed architecture, and hates screens, I do not hesitate to denounce him as a liar, for one is inseparable from the other, and *more*, inseparable from *Catholic arrangement in any style*, Byzantine, Norman, Pointed, or debased. We have now to contend for the great principles of Catholic antiquity,—tradition and reverence against modern development and display. It is not a struggle for taste or ornament, but a contention for *vital principles*. There is a most intimate connection between the externals of religion and the faith itself; and it is scarcely possible to preserve the interior faith in the doctrine of the holy eucharist if all exterior reverence and respect is to be abolished.

"There is no higher act in the Christian religion," says Father Le Brun, "than the Sacrifice of the Mass; the greater portion of the other sacraments, and nearly all the offices and ceremonies of the church, are only the means or the preparation to celebrate or participate in it worthily." Such being the case, it is but natural that the place where this most holy sacrifice is to be offered up, should be set apart and railed off from less sacred portions of the church, and we find this to have been the case in all ages, in all styles, and in all countries professing the Catholic faith down to a comparatively very recent period, when in many places all feelings of sanctity, tradition, and reverence, seemed to have been superseded by ignorant innovation and love of change.

It will be shown in this work that the idea of room-worship, and the all-seeing principles, is a perfect novelty. Those indeed who would make the mass *a sight*, are only to be compared to the innovators of the 16th century, who made it essential to be *heard*; those who compiled the Book of Common Prayer converted the mass into all-hearing service; this was the great object of the vernacular change, that people might *hear* the priest; they were to be edified by what he *said*, more than what he *did*; the sacrificial act was merged into the audible recitation of prayers and exhortations; for this reason the altars, in the reign of Edward the Sixth, were to be moved down from their eastern position to the entrance of the chancel, to enable the people to hear; this led to the demolition of stone altars and the substitution of tables. For this reason the whole congregation crowd into the choirs of the cathedrals, leaving the rest of the church deserted. For this reason, in large parochial churches, the chancel has been often entirely cut off, and a portion of the nave glazed in and reduced to such a size that the people could hear the clergyman; these were all natural consequences of the change of principle consequent on the translation of the mass, and the altered nature of its celebration. That churches are now built after the old tradition for the service of the separated portion of the English Church, is purely owing to an internal revival of Catholic feelings and traditions in that body: the cause is a return to Catholic truth and reverence; the effect is the erection of churches in accordance with those feelings. It has been a charge and reproach made by Catholics against their separated countrymen, that the old fabrics were unsuited to their service, and unquestionably, on the principle that it was essential for *every one to hear*, they were so. But I will ask these new-fashioned men if it is indispensable for *every one to see*, how much better are they adapted for modern Catholic rites? They become as unfit for one as the other, for it is unquestionable, that comparatively very few persons in these cruciform churches could obtain a view of the altar, and this *independent of any screen-work*, the disposition of the pillars intersecting and shutting out all those who are stationed in the aisles and transepts.

I have always imagined that one great distinction between the Protestant and Catholic services was this, that the former was essentially a *hearing* service, at which only a comparatively few persons could assist, while at the latter many thousands, or, indeed, hundreds of thousands could unite in one great act of adoration and praise, concentrating their thoughts and intentions with the priest who is offering at God's altar, although he is far shut off from their vision.

Real Protestants have always built rooms for their worship, or walled up the old churches, when they have fallen into their possession, into four or five distinct spaces, as in Scotland. But the separated church of England, though Protestant in position, in name, and in practice, has retained so much of the old traditions in her service, and is linked by so many ties to older and better times, that she naturally turns back to them with affection and reverence, and seeks, as far as her maimed rites and fettered position will admit, to restore the departed glory of the sanctuary. Few persons are aware that the choirs of three of the English cathedrals were completely restalled, and after the old arrangements, by the munificence of churchmen in the seventeenth century; moreover, the completion of some towers and extensive works date from the same period. It is a consoling fact, that the cathedrals of England retain more of their old Catholic arrangements and fittings than most of those on the continent: and as regards the fabricks, they have suffered less injury, and have preserved their original character most wonderfully. Architecturally, we must certainly admit that the Anglicans have been good tenants of the old fabricks; we must not test them by the works of preceding centuries, but by the corresponding period; and when we reflect on the debased state of design and art that prevailed, even in those countries which were nominally exclusively Catholic, we may be thankful that our great religious edifices have been so well handed down to our own times, when the recognition of their beauty and grandeur is daily increasing.[2] I have dilated on this subject, for if the lingering remains

---

[2] I trust to be able before long to put forth an impartial statement relative to the destruction of Catholic edifices and ornaments consequent on the change of religion in England. After the most patient investigation, I have been compelled to adopt the conclusion, that the most fearful acts of destruction and spoliation were committed by men who had

of Catholic traditions which have been so imperfectly preserved since the separation of England in the sixteenth century, have yet produced such edifying results, how much more have we reason to expect from those who should possess them in all their fullness! and how heart-rending, how deplorable, how scandalous is it to behold (as, sad to say, we have now fearful examples) even priests of the very temple combining, by word and deed, to break down the carved work of the sanctuary, and destroying the barriers erected by ancient reverence and faith!

But to return, I cannot too strongly impress on the minds of my readers that the very *vitals* of Catholic architecture are assailed by the opponents of screens.

Those who complain of not being able to see in a Pointed church should have assisted at an ancient service in a Roman basilica; the altar surrounded by pillars sustaining veils and curtains, and covered by a ciborium, was placed in *front* of the celebrant, of whom nothing could be discerned by the congregation except an occasional glimpse of his head; the space behind the altar was reserved for the bishop and his presbyters, while in front was the choir for those who sung, walled round to a considerable height, averaging five feet, and within, or occasionally outside, this space, were the ambones for the epistle and gospel, marble rostrums, ascended by steps, and usually of large dimensions; moreover, the basilicæ were constructed with aisles, like pointed churches, so that not one-tenth part of the congregation could have seen either the celebrant or the mensæ of the altar. And although it does not appear that the Latin church has purposely excluded the sight of the altar from the people, yet from the beginning the canonical arrangement of her sacred edifices has had the practical effect of cutting off its view from a very large portion of the assisting faithful.

Christians of the present time have but little idea of the solemnity of the ancient worship of the Catholic church; ordained ministers were alone permitted to fill the humblest offices about the sanctuary, every object connected with the sacred rites were considered deserving of the most loving care; even in the very early ages, the vessels of the altar were usually of precious metals, and studded with jewels. The books of the holy gospels were written in golden text on purple vellum, bound in plates of silver encasing ivory diptychs, and deposited in portable shrines, like relics. Though all this should fill us with admiration, there is nothing to excite surprise, when we reflect on the very sacred nature of the Christian mysteries—no sign typical and prophetic, as under the Mosaic law, but our blessed Lord truly present and abiding in the temple in the holy sacrament of the altar,—it is by no means wonderful that the Christian worship should assume a form of solemnity formerly unknown, and we are only astounded that with the perpetuation of the

not only been educated in the ancient faith, but who were contented externally to profess its doctrines. I had originally fallen into popular errors on these matters in some of my early publications, and it is but an act of justice to affix the odium of the sacrilege on those who were really guilty. I feel quite satisfied that one of the most urgent wants of the time is a real statement of the occurrences connected with the establishment of Protestantism and the loss of the ancient faith; of course, I have to treat the subject in an architectural view, but still I trust to bring forward many facts that may lead to a better understanding and more charity on both sides, for we may all exclaim, "Patres nostri pecaverunt et non sunt, *et nos iniquitates eorum portavimus.*"

doctrine the practice of external solemnity should have so lamentably become decayed in the latter times; indeed, so sacred, so awful, so mysterious is the sacrifice of the mass, that if men were seriously to reflect on what it really consists, so far from advocating mere rooms for its celebration, they would hasten to restore the reverential arrangements of Catholic antiquity, and instead of striving for front seats and first places, they would hardly feel worthy to occupy the remotest corner of the temple. The form and arrangement of the ancient churches originated from the deepest feelings of reverence; the altar, or place of sacrifice, was accessible only to those who ministered, it was enclosed by pillars and veils; the sanctuary was veiled, the choir was enclosed, and the faithful adored at a respectful distance. All this, and the custom of every succeeding century, is in utter opposition to the modern all-seeing principle, and which, if it is carried out, ends in an absurd conclusion; for if it be essential for every worshipper to see, even a *level room* would not answer the purpose, and the floor must be raised like an amphitheatre to elevate the receding *spectators*, for unless the people be thus raised, they form a far greater barrier than any screen-work; and even at St. Peter's itself, when the Pope celebrates, there is a living screen of Swiss troops and noble guards that effectually shuts out the sight of what is going on, except to those taking part in the functions, or a favoured few, who by means of gold or interest are seated in raised loggia. If religious ceremonies are to be regarded as spectacles they should be celebrated in regular theatres, which have been expressly invented for the purpose of accommodating great assemblages of persons to hear and see well. It has been most justly said, that there is no legitimate halting-place between Catholic doctrine and positive infidelity, and I am quite certain that there is none between a church built on Christian tradition and symbolism and Covent Garden Theatre with its pit, boxes, and gallery.[3] It is only by putting the question in this forcible contrast that persons can really understand the danger of these new notions, or the lengths to which they may eventually lead; and I trust it may be the means of raising a feeling of the greatest repugnance to them in the hearts of every true Catholic.

As regards screens, I believe there are no portions of church architecture the origin and intention of which are less understood, and I have seen most absurd and contradictory arguments brought forward in their defence as well as by their assailants; they have originated from a natural as well as a symbolical intention,—it is a natural principle to enclose any portion of a building or space which is set apart from public use and access, and when such a boundary is erected round the place of sacrifice in a church, it teaches the faithful to reverence the seat of the holy mysteries, and to worship in humility.

From the earliest times the choirs and sanctuaries of the Christian churches were separated off from the rest of the building by open metal-work and dwarf marble walls, and at the present day, in those churches where the old screen-work has been destroyed by debased tastes or revolutionary violence, it has invariably been replaced by high iron railings, as indispensably necessary for the order and discipline of the church; and though these railings are meagre in effect and prison-like in appearance, they are screens to all intents and purposes, and serve like

[3] I have been credibly informed, that an amphitheatre was deliberately proposed, a few years since, as the best form of a Catholic church for London.

their more ornamental prototypes to exclude unauthorized persons from the sacred enclosures.

The choirs of the early Christian churches, which were all frequented by the people, were enclosed by open screens, like trellis-work, usually made of brass, and this principle has descended through all ages in churches destined for *parochial worship* and *the use of the people*, while in cathedral, collegiate, and conventual churches, which were intended more especially for the use of ecclesiastics, the solid screens were invariable, not only across the nave but round the choir, so that the canons and religious were completely enclosed. The introduction of these close screens was coeval with the commencement of the long offices, and were positively necessary for those who were compelled to remain so many hours in choir, and who would have been unable to resist the cold if exposed to the free passage of the currents of air which prevail in these large edifices.[4]

But, like every object generated in necessity, the church soon turned them to a most edifying account, and while the great screen was adorned with the principal events of our Lord's life and passion, surmounted by the great rood, the lateral walls were carved with edifying sculptures and sacred histories, many of which still remain, as at Notre Dame, Paris, Amiens, Chartres, Auch, &c. I do not think that the theory, which some writers have advanced, of these *close* screens being erected to increase the mystery of the celebration, and to procure greater respect for the sacrifice, is tenable; the mass is not more holy in one church or one altar than another, and it is most certain that no parochial churches, built as such, ever had close screens, but always open ones; and, indeed, we very often find altars erected outside these close screens of cathedral and conventual churches, for the benefit of the people, as will be seen by the plates given in this work, which would involve a complete contradiction in principle, supposing the high altar to be hid on symbolical grounds. The *close* screens belong properly to the choir rather than the altar, as in many Italian churches served by religious, the clergy sat behind the screen, while the altar is partly without, so that the celebration served for both the religious and the people.

At Durham Abbey, the Jesus altar was outside of the great screen; and at St. Alban's Abbey, in the screen which traverses the nave, there are the evident marks of an altar which doubtless served for the parochial mass.

It will be seen from these remarks that close screens, as a principle, are only suitable for churches intended for cathedral chapters or conventual and collegiate bodies; and they are certainly most unsuitable for any churches to be erected in this country under existing circumstances, where the limited extent of means and number of the clergy render it necessary for all services to be available for the faithful in general, and the bishops' churches, like the original basilicæ, to be in a manner parochial.

But as regards open screens the case is widely different; they existed under the form of trellis (opere reticulato) in the oldest churches, and, in succeeding centuries not only was every chancel and choir enclosed by them, but each chapel, and

[4] These enclosures were also to prevent the distraction which large bodies of people moving about the church might occasion to the ecclesiastics.

even altar; they were to be found in every parochial church, either of metal, stone, or wood; in Germany, Flanders, and the North, metal was the usual material, but in England and France stone and wood, while in Italy and the South they were usually composed partly of marble and partly of metal. But their use was universal, they commenced many centuries *before the introduction of pointed architecture*, and *they have survived its decline*; in fact, they belong to the first principles of Catholic *reverence and order*, and *not to any particular style*, though, like everything else connected with the church, they attained their greatest beauty in the mediæval period.

The church of San Michele, at Florence, contains an altar erected in the fourteenth century, in honour of a venerated picture of the Blessed Virgin; it is a most interesting example of a detached altar surrounded by a screen. Like all the Italian mediæval works, it is exquisitely beautiful in detail, and admirable in the sculptured enrichments; it is entirely surrounded by a screen, partly composed of bronze and partly of marble, divided in open panels of pointed tracery; this supports a cresting, with prickets for tapers, and at the four angles are images of angels bearing metal candlesticks of elegant design. In order to convey a more perfect idea of this beautiful and decorated altar, I have figured it among the illustrations. In Ciampini's great work, "Vetera Monimenta," are plates of some of the altars which stood in old St. Peter's Church, at Rome, enclosed by brass screens, surrounded by standards for lights; and as a proof of the extent of this traditional enclosure of altars, when Antwerp Cathedral was restored to Catholic worship, after its pillage by the Calvinists in the sixteenth century, there not only was a great marble screen and rood loft restored across the choir, but a new range of altars having been set up against the pillars of the nave, each altar was enclosed by an open brass screen about six feet high, supported on a marble base, as may be most distinctly seen in a view of the church painted at the time by Peter Neefs, still preserved at Bicton House, near Sidmouth, and from which I have made the drawing etched in this work. I consider these authorities rather important, as when this church was restored for the Catholic worship all feeling for pointed design had been superseded by Italian; but change of detail had not then produced change of sentiment, and I shall clearly show that Catholic traditions, in this respect, have survived all changes of form and ornament.

It is, therefore, these open railings, or screen-work, for which we contend as an essential characteristic of Catholic reverence in the enclosure of chancels, chapels, and altars; practically, they prevent any irreverence or intrusion in the sacred places at those times when no celebration or office is going on; and symbolically, they impress on the minds of the faithful the great sanctity of all connected with the sacrifice of the altar, and that, like the vicinity of the "burning bush," the ground itself is holy. Wherever this screen or enclosures have been removed, as in some modernized churches of Italy and France, distressing irreverence has been the consequence; and, on more than one occasion, I have seen an altar turned into a hat-stand within a few minutes after the holy sacrifice had been offered up upon it, while animals defile the frontals, and lazzaroni lounge on the steps.

These screens serve also for a most edifying purpose; while the principal one across the chancel or choir sustains the great rood, with its attendant imagery and ornaments, the lateral enclosures are surmounted by ranges of metal standards for lights, to burn on great feasts, while the mouldings and bratishings are enriched with texts and sacred devices.

The rest of this work may be considered only as a justification and proof of what I have advanced in this brief essay, viz.—1st. That open screens and enclosures of choirs and chancels have existed from the earliest known period of Christian churches down to the present century, that they form an essential part of Catholic tradition and reverence, and that no church intended for Catholic worship can be complete without them. 2nd. That their introduction belongs to no particular period or style, and that their partial disuse was not consequent on the decline of pointed architecture, but to the decay of reverence for the sacred mysteries themselves, as I have found screens of all styles and dates. 3rd. That closed screens are only now suited to conventual and collegiate churches in this country, the cathedrals being required for the worship of the people, from whom the view of the altar has never been purposely concealed. 4th. That those who oppose the revival and continuance of open screens are not only enemies of Catholic traditions and practices, but the grounds of their objections militate as strongly against every symbolic form and arrangement in ecclesiastical architecture, and, therefore, till they retract their opposition they are practically insulting the traditions of the church, impeding the restoration of reverence and solemnity, and injuring the progress of religion.

OF THE ENCLOSURE OF CHOIRS, FROM THE EARLY AGES OF THE CHURCH DOWN TO THE PRESENT TIME.

I⊤ is most certain (writes the learned Thiers) that in the three first centuries there were churches, that is to say, places set apart for the faithful to meet in prayer and assist at the holy sacrifice; but we have no record respecting the internal arrangements of those places, which often were mere rooms in private houses, hence it is impossible to say whether any separation existed in them between the people and the clergy.

But from the time of Constantine's conversion, it is beyond doubt that the choirs were divided off from the other portion of the church by veils or screens. Eusebius describes the choir of the Church of the Apostles, erected by Constantine at Constantinople, as enclosed by screens, or trellis-work, marvellously wrought.—"Interiorem ædis partem undique in ambitum circumductam, *reticulato opere* ex ære et auro affabre facto convestivit."

The same writer thus speaks of the choir of the Church of Tyre, built and consecrated by the Bishop Paulinus:—"Porro sanctuario hoc modo absoluto et perfecto, thronisque quibusdam in altissimo loco ad Præsidum ecclesiæ honorem collocatis, et subselliis præterea undique ordine dispositis, decore eximieque exornato, altarique undique tanquam Sancto Sanctorum in medio sanctuarii sito, ista rursus, ut a plebe et multitudine eo non posset accedi, cancellis ex ligno fabricatis circumdedit, qui adeo artificiosa solertia ad summum elaborati sunt, ut mirabile spectaculum intuentibus exhibeant."

The emperor Theodosius divides the church into three parts:—"Sacro sanctum Altare *Cancellis Clausum*, quadratum Templi oratorium murorum ambitu circumseptum, et locum residuum usque ad ecclesiæ fores exteriores." And St. Paulinus, Bishop of Nola, describes three doors in the screens of the Church of St. Felix.

Trinaque Cancellis currentibus ostia pandunt.

Among the decrees of the Second Council of Tours, in 557, it is ordered that lay persons are not to enter the chancel which is divided off by screens, except to receive the holy communion:—"Ut Laici secus altare, quo sancta mysteria celebrantur, inter Clericos, tam ad vigilias, quam ad Missas, stare penitus non præsumant; sed pars illa *quæ a Cancellis versus Altare dividitur*, Choris tantum psallentium pateat Clericorum. Ad orandum vero et communicandum laicis et feminis, sicut mos est, pateant Sancta Sanctorum."

St. Germanus, patriarch of Constantinople, thus explains the intention and meaning of the choir screens:—"Cancelli locum orationis designant, quojusque extrinsecus populus accedit. Intrinsecus autem sunt Sancta Sanctorum solis Sacerdotibus pervia. Sunt autem revera ad piam memoriam *Cancelli ænei*,[5] nequis simpliciter et temere ingrediatur."

The space enclosed by these screens in those churches where the aisles extended round the choir was entered by three double gates, those to the west, at the lower end of the choir, were called "the holy doors," the others were placed between the choir and the sanctuary, on the epistle and gospel sides. But in smaller churches, where the chancel alone forms the eastern extremity, there was only one pair of gates, or holy doors, at the west, and this most ancient arrangement has continued down to the present day, even in churches that have been fitted up with modern iron railings.

From the authorities above quoted, which are some cited by Father Thiers, in his treatise, Sur le Cloture des Chœurs, it will be seen that open screens existed from the earliest erection of churches, and that they were composed of wood or metal, most frequently brass. This style of enclosure prevailed universally in all classes of churches till the end of the twelfth century, when, in the cathedral and collegiate churches, they were altered into solid walls, in the manner and for the reasons before described in the introduction to this work.

THE CONSTITUTIONS OF S. CHARLES BORROMEO.

In the "Constitutions" of the great St. Charles Borromeo, which were of course subsequent to the Council of Trent, are the following interesting decrees relative to the enclosure of altars:—

Of the Choir.

The place of the choir (since it ought to be by the high altar, whether it surround it from before, as the ancient custom was, or it be behind, because either the site of the church, or the position of the altar, or the custom of the place so require) being separated from the space occupied by the people (as the ancient structures and the nature of the discipline show) and surrounded by screens, ought to extend so far, both in length and breadth, where the space of the site allows of it (even to the form of a semicircle, or some other shape, according to the character of the church or chapel, in the judgment of the architect), as to correspond fitly in capaciousness, as well as in becoming adornment, to the dignity of the church, and the number of the clergy.

Of the High Altar.

The high altar ought to be so placed as that there shall be between the lowest step to it and *the screen-work by which it is, or is to be, fenced*, a space of eight cubits, and even more where possible, and the size of the church requires it for its proper adornment.

[5] The custom of using brass for the material of choir screens is to be traced to a very late period, as at St. Gatier, at Tours; Cathedral, Rouen; and in many of the Flemish cathedrals.

OF THE JUBÉ, OR ROOD LOFT.

It was the custom of the primitive church, and long afterwards, to sing the Epistle and Gospel from two stone pulpits placed at the lower end of the choir, from whence they could be conveniently heard by the people; and from this reason they were termed "ambones." Of these, many examples are remaining in the ancient basilicas, especially at San Lorenzo, San Clemente, &c., at Rome. These pulpits were also used for chanting the lessons of the Divine Office, and from the reader asking a blessing before commencing with, Jubé Domine Benedicite, they were commonly called "jubés," which name was retained when those pulpits were exalted into a lofty gallery reaching across the choir.

It is difficult to affix the precise period when the transverse jubés, or rood lofts, were first erected, but they must be of very great antiquity, as that of St. Sophia at Constantinople was large enough to enable the emperors to be crowned in it, a function which would require space for a considerable number of persons.

The French kings always ascended the jubé of Rheims Cathedral at their coronation; and on the accession of Charles X., as the ancient rood loft had been demolished, a temporary one was erected for the solemnity of his coronation.

These jubés were usually erected on a solid wall to the choir, and pillars with open arches towards the nave; and under them there was usually one or more altars for the parochial mass.

They were usually ascended by two staircases, either in circular turrets[6] or carried up in the thickness of the wall, which was generally the case in England.

Occasionally we find altars were erected in the lofts, under the foot of the cross; such was the case at Vienne, in the Church of St. Maurice, where the parochial altar was in the centre of the rood loft, and the Blessed Sacrament was also reserved there Sub titulo crucis.

OF THE FURNITURE OF THE ROOD LOFTS.

1.— The GREAT CRUCIFIX and ROOD, with its attendant images, stood always in the centre of the loft.

The cross was usually framed of timber, richly carved, painted, and gilt; at its extremities the four Evangelists were depicted, and frequently on the reverse the four doctors of the church. The Evangelists were sometimes represented as sitting figures in the act of writing, but more frequently under the form of the apocalyptical symbols. The extremities of the cross usually terminated in fleur-de-lys, and its sides were foliated or crocketed.

The Blessed Virgin and St. John were the almost invariable accompaniments of the crucifix, but cherubim were occasionally added. As these Roods were of great weight, their support was assisted by wrought-iron chains, depending from the great stone arch on the entrance to the choir and chancel, and the staples for these chains are frequently to be seen in churches from which the Roods have been

[6] The only instance I have found in England of circular staircases to a rood loft, inside the church, is at Ely, before the old alterations of the choir.

removed.

2.—LECTERNS for the Epistle, Gospel, and Lessons. These lecterns were either moveable brass stands, like those in choirs, or marble desks, forming part of the masonry of the design: these are still left in many churches on the continent. Those at the Frairi at Venice are most beautiful, and, to come nearer home, in a rood loft at Tatershall Church is a curiously-moulded stone desk for the reader of the lessons.

3.—CORONELS and STANDARDS for LIGHTS.

Coronels of silver or other metal were suspended on all the great rood lofts, and filled with lighted tapers, on solemn feasts. The maintenance of the rood lights was a frequent and somewhat heavy item in the old churchwardens' accounts, as will be seen by extracts published in this work.

At Bourges there were twenty-four brass basins, with prickets for tapers, which the bishops used to supply at their own cost.

The Blessed Sacrament was usually exposed from the rood loft. The exposition on the high altar of Lyons Cathedral was mentioned as occurring for the first time in the year 1701. All the solemn expositions at Rouen took place from one of the altars under the rood loft, and there is every reason to believe that the Blessed Sacrament was usually exposed either on the rood lofts or the altars attached to them; but these expositions were only at considerable intervals of time, and only permitted on some great and urgent occasion, and they were then conducted with the greatest possible solemnity, as may be seen in the account given by De Moleon of the exposition of the Blessed Sacrament at the Cathedral, Rouen. Branches of trees were commonly set up in these rood lofts at Christmas and Whitsuntide, and they were also occasionally decorated with flowers.

The principal use of these lofts was for the solemn singing of the Epistle and Gospel; but, as I have said before, the lessons and the great antiphons, &c., were also chanted from them. In the Greek Church, the deacon read the diptychs from the rood loft, and formerly warned the catechumens and the penitents to depart before the mass, crying out Sancta Sanctis! The fronts of the old rood lofts were frequently most richly decorated with paintings or sculptures of sacred history, divided into panels or niches, surmounted by a rich bratishing of open tracery-work and foliage.

THE ROOD BEAM.—In the generality of wooden screens, the breastsumer of the screen forms the beam on which the rood is fixed and tennanted; but there are instances where the beam is fixed at some height above the top, as at Little Malvern, the intervening space being filled in with some tracery, or enrichment. The position of this beam gave rise to a very ludicrous mistake on the part of one of the recent screen opponents, who cited this church as an example of a mere beam to sustain a rood without a screen; but unfortunately for his argument, the screen itself is still standing beneath, in its original position. In Italy, at Milan, Sienna, Ovieto, and several of the larger churches, there is only a beam sustaining the rood, with images of the Blessed Virgin and St. John. Some of them are ornamental in design, but I do not think any of them older than the sixteenth century. There are several examples in France, but all comparatively modern; but in the Domkirche, at Lubeck, there is a most remarkable example of a rood beam, that merits a particular description. The beam itself is composed of a great many pieces of timber, deeply moulded and carved, and enriched with pendent tracery and crocketed braces. It stretches across the nave in the westernmost arch, on a line with transept, the rood screen being across the easternmost one.

The cross is covered with open tracery, and crocketed; each crocket is an expanding flower, from which the bust of a prophet issues, bearing a scroll with a prophecy relative to our Lord's passion. The same images are carved at the extremities of the four great quatrefoils, containing the emblems of the Evangelists. The images of the Blessed Virgin, St. John, St. Mary Magdalen, and the bishop at whose cost the work was set up, are placed on the beam: the two latter are kneeling. Between these, the dead are seen arising from their graves; and in either angle, on a corbel, an angel of justice and mercy. Beyond these, on the piers of the church, are two images of Adam and Eve; and a host of smaller angels and images complete the personages of this most extraordinary work. Some of the images are rather barbarous, but the foliage and details are exquisitely wrought, and the whole design is most striking and original.

There are rood beams at Nuremberg, but the originality of that in St. Lawrence's Church is rather doubtful,—though the antiquity of the rood itself is certain. Each arm of the cross ramifies into three branches, at the extremities of which are angels, with chalices, and on the top branch a pelican.

Gervase, the monk of Canterbury, in his description of that cathedral, makes the following statement: Under the great tower was erected the altar of the holy cross, and a screen which separated the tower from the nave: a *beam* was laid across, and upon the middle of this beam a great cross, with images of the Blessed Virgin and St. John, and two cherubim.

There is a rood beam of some antiquity at the church of Séran, near Gisors. It is placed across the westernmost arch of the central tower. And the same may be remarked in several of the Normandy churches; but in some cases they stand considerably above the top of the screen; while in others the screens have been removed at a very recent period, probably that of the great revolution.

From the Instructiones Fabricæ of S. Charles Borromeo.

Under the vaulted arch of the chancel in every church, especially parochial churches, let a cross, having thereon the image of Christ, devoutly and becomingly made of wood, or any other material, be exposed, and conveniently placed.

But if, on account of the great depression of the arch or vaulting, it cannot be placed so well there, then let it be put up against the wall, over the arch, under the ceiling; or let it be placed over the chancel door.

ON SCREENS IN ITALY AND SPAIN.

I COMMENCE with Italy, first, because it has been the fountain from whence Catholic truth has flowed to other parts of Christendom, and secondly, as I believe it is a very general delusion that screens formed no part of the fittings of a Roman church.

As an overwhelming contradiction to this often-repeated error, I produce a representation of the great screen in old St. Peter's, from the most irrefragable authority,[7] from which it will be seen that a *double* marble wall was erected, about six feet high, and twelve feet apart, that on these walls stood twelve porphyry pillars, supporting a transverse cornice surmounted with standards for lights. Moreover, at the neck of these pillars, under the cap, rods were extended for the suspension of lamps, which were kept perpetually burning in honour of the Apostles, whose relics lay beneath the high altar.

This altar, as will be seen by the plan, stood considerably within the screen, surrounded by pillars, and covered by a ciborium. The back of the altar is turned towards the nave, with a cross and candlesticks upon it, and must have effectually concealed the celebrant from the people; behind all this is seen the great apse, with the cathedra for the pope, mosaic ceiling, and usual decorations.

This is the most important authority for the use of screens in the ancient Roman church; and the dignity and sanctity of the old basilica of St. Peter was so great, that it would be naturally considered as the type for other churches; moreover, if we except the details which belong to the early period of its erection, it is a perfect type of a Pointed screen,—convert the twelve pillars into shafts, surmount them with arches, and terminate them by a bratishing, and we have a work of the mediæval period. It is also exceedingly interesting to observe that this screen is surmounted by standards for wax tapers, and many lamps were suspended

[7] Ciampini, de Sacris Ædificiis, p. xvi. Fontana, Templum Vaticanum, p. 89. Pistolezi, Il Vaticano Descritto, vol. 7, p. 57. From Professor Willis's History of Canterbury Cathedral:—"Screen of old St. Peter's, at Rome.—In front of the steps were placed twelve columns of Parian marble, arranged in two rows; these were of a spiral form, and decorated with sculpture of vine leaves: the bases were connected by lattice-work of metal, or by walls of marble breast high. The entrance was between the central pillars, where the cancelli, or lattices, were formed into doors, which gave access to the presbytery as well as the confessionary. Above these columns were laid beams, or entablatures, upon which were placed images, candelabra, and other decorations; and, indeed, the successive Popes seem to have lavished every species of decoration in gold, silver, and marble-work upon this enclosure and the crypt below. The entire height, measured to the top of the entablature, was about thirty feet; the columns, with the connecting lattices and entablatures, formed, in fact, *the screen of the chancel.*"

from it. The most modern screens of the seventeenth and eighteenth century still preserve these features, and the traditional arrangement has lasted from the reign of the emperor Constantine down to our time. It will be seen by the plate which represents the screen, that the altar is covered with an elevated ciborium, raised on four pillars, connected by rods, from which veils of silk and precious stuffs were suspended. It may be useful to remark, that, although as I have before said, the altar itself was never shut off purposely from the sight of the people, yet it is most certain that all altars were provided with these veils or curtains, which were closely drawn during the consecration. There is especial mention of the gifts of such curtains by the early popes to the altars of churches in Rome;[8] and though this rite has been long disused, yet the lateral curtains, suspended on rods, which still hang in many continental churches, are remains of the ancient reverential practice. It is greatly to be desired that these ciborium altars were more generally revived in our times, especially for the reservation of the holy sacrament. Their vaulted coverings are not only most majestic in appearance, but they are practically useful in preventing the deposition of dust on the altar and tabernacle. In all cases, side curtains should be retained for altars in lateral chapels, as they preserve the celebrant from distraction, and protect the tapers, &c., from currents of air. But to answer these ends, it is essential that the curtains should be suspended nearly at right angles to the reredos, and not expanded flat against the walls, as may be seen in some churches of our own time.

THE SISTINE CHAPEL SCREEN.

This screen, which is still standing, is probably not older than the sixteenth century. It is composed of an elevated basement of marble, about five feet high, and divided above this into compartments, by square pillars of marble, supporting an entablature, and the spaces between them being filled by a bronze grating of crossing bars, making a total height of above 12 feet. On the top of the entablature are metal standards for tapers.

Father Bonanni, who wrote in the seventeenth century, describes the chapel as arranged in the following manner:—1. The altar. 2. The pope's throne. 3. The benches for the cardinals and prelates. 4. An enclosed space for the religious and officers of the pope's court. 5. A sort of balustrade which separates these portions from the laity: at the top of this balustrade are placed four, six, or seven tapers, according to the solemnity of the time.

The term balustrade has been usually applied by old writers to screens, and must not be understood in the modern acceptation, of signifying a sort of rail hand high; in this instance we have a clear proof to the contrary, for the screen termed a balustrade is still standing, and, with the exception of the style of pillars and mouldings, is very similar to those erected in Pointed churches. Trevoux, in his great dictionary, has the following explanation of the word: "Balustre also signi-

---

[8] Anastasius, in his Lives of the Popes, mentions Sergius I., Gregory III., Adrian I., Leo III., Pascal I., Gregory IV., Sergius II., Leo IV., and Nicholas I., as munificent donors of costly veils for the altars of various churches in Rome, as may be seen at length in Thiers's Traité des Autels, chap. xiv.

fies those small *pillars* to shut off the alcove in a room, or the chancel of a church or chapel. Columellæ, Cancelli, &c." In this sense they are always to be understood when mentioned by old writers in reference to church architecture. Low balustrades, or rails, were unknown to antiquity. The enclosures were always of a sufficient height to prevent persons getting over them, and the low rails round altars, are, in England, a pure Protestant introduction, and originated in the necessity of preventing the gross irreverence offered by the Puritan party to the holy tables, on which they frequently sat during the sermon. If the word balustrade as used by French and Italian writers, be not thoroughly understood, it must lead to a misconception of the old arrangements. Pistolezi, in his great work on the Vatican, describes this screen as a balustrade; his words are as follows:—"La Capella—e divisa in due spartamenti, il minore, che della Porta alla *Balustrata* de marmore si estende, *serve per i Laici*," &c.

THE QUIRINAL CHAPEL.

Has a wall in the same position as the screen of the Sistine chapel, about five feet high, surmounted by pillars, bearing candelabra for large wax tapers, but the spaces between these are open. This was set up in the pontificate of Pius VI.

SAN CLEMENTE.

The marble enclosure of the choir is four feet six inches high; the floor of this choir is two steps above the nave. Between this choir and the sanctuary is a cross wall of marble, six feet high, with an opening in the centre, through which only the back of the altar can be discerned, as the basilica is turned to the west. It will be readily perceived by these arrangements, that although no ornamental screen-work existed, yet, practically, the sanctuary is far more shut out than in Pointed parochial churches, where the solid panelling rarely exceeds three feet six inches; and it must be admitted, that, if the first few feet were built up solid, as at San Clemente, it is a matter of little consequence, as regards facilities of seeing, whether this base is surmounted by open work, or terminated by a cornice.

The original fittings and choral arrangements of the greater part of the ancient churches at Rome have been entirely modernized, with a view to their embellishment, during the revived Pagan period. Indeed, this city has been singularly unfortunate. During the prevalence of Christian art, it was almost deserted, and even the Popes resided at Avignon, in a pointed palace of stupendous dimensions and design. But on their return, the new and corrupt ideas of art had arisen, and so much money was expended in rebuilding and altering the ancient edifices, that Rome possesses far less interesting ecclesiastical buildings than many comparatively small cities of Italy, and it is impossible to form the least idea of the beauty of Italian mediæval art, without visiting those places that have had the advantages of poverty and neglect, and the consequent preservation of the ancient and appropriate fittings.

THE BASILICA OF ST. NEREI AND ACHILLE, ROME.[9]

This remarkable screen is of marble, about seven feet high, cut like a panelled wall. A flight of steps ascends on each side behind the screen, to an elevated platform, from which rise the steps and ciborium of the altar; on this same level the Epistle and Gospel were sung by the deacon and sub-deacon, from marble desks enriched with carvings, and fixed on the entablature of the screens. There are two twisted candlesticks for tapers, and it is probable that originally there were a greater number. The altar, as usual, has its back turned towards the people; so that this truly ancient and interesting church is in diametrical opposition to the all-seeing principle of modern times.

I have figured a curious example of an iron screen from a painting in the cathedral of Sienna, by Pinturicchio. I imagine this sort of metal trellis screens to have been very common in the Italian churches.[10]

We next proceed to Florence, where the remains of mediæval architecture are far more extensive and interesting than at Rome. The choir of the cathedral is immediately under the dome; an octagon subasement supported a screen of the Doric order, covered with sculptures and bas-reliefs. This was only removed a few years since, and, in consequence of its removal, the canons, in order to preserve themselves from the cold air, usually officiate during the winter months in a glazed chapel, very like a large counting-house, that has been erected on the north side of the church. It is, I believe, practically impossible to keep choir in this church without a screen.

SANTA CROCE.

In this church many of the old screens yet remain. They are for the most part composed of metal trellis-work, supported by wrought uprights, and terminated by open bratishing. Those on the north side are quite perfect, and evidently coeval with the fabric.

SAN MICHELE.

The altar of the church San Michele, which was erected in a building originally a corn-market, out of devotion to a picture of our Blessed Lady, that was depicted against one of the pillars. It is surrounded by a superb screen of marble and bronze, which will be better understood by referring to the plate, on which it is figured. The execution of the sculpture of this altar is most admirable, and the minutest details are finished with extreme delicacy and care, and many of the panels are enriched with precious stones and jaspers. The upper part of the screen supports a richly-moulded brass trough, to receive the drippings of the numerous tapers offered upon this altar, and for which standards with prickets are disposed

---

[9] There are five illustrations of this church in an interesting Italian work, entitled Monumenti della Religione Cristiana.

[10] These pictures are all engraved in a work entitled Raccolta delle più celebri Pitture di Sienna.

above each mullion or division of the screen. The whole is in the most perfect state, and offers a splendid example of mediæval Italian art.

SAN PETRONIO, BOLOGNA.

The nave of this gigantic and noble church is alone completed. The choir at the eastern end is therefore but a temporary erection in the two last bays. Several of the side chapels are enclosed by Pointed screens, coeval with the erection of the church. They are composed partly of wood, and partly of marble and metal; but they are elaborate and lofty, and quite of the same character as those of the northern churches.

PADUA.

The church of San Antonio has a large screen and rood loft, of cinque-cento-work, at the entrance of the choir, which is also surrounded by screen-work, and another screen, of a much older date, with open arches and tracery-work executed in marble, divides off the chapel of S. Felice from the main body of the church. The arrangement of the choir of this remarkable church is very similar to that which prevailed in the French cathedrals; and some of the churches in Venice bear a very close resemblance to the Flemish ecclesiastical buildings.

The chapel of Santa Maria dell' Arena, in the same city, remains nearly in its original state, and exhibits a very curious example of choral arrangement. The stalls partly return on each side of the entrance, and are backed by stone walls about four feet high on the inside, and seven on the outside; the space between them is ascended by steps, and forms a platform or ambo for the chanting of the Gospel and Epistles, for which purpose an iron and a marble desk, both of the fourteenth century, still remain. These form a screen to the choir, and serve as dosells or reredoses to two altars which are placed against them. There are no appearances of there ever having been any screen-work above these, but all above a solid wall seven feet high is of small consequence as regards facilities of seeing for those in the nave. This chapel was not, however, parochial, but erected for the use of a confraternity.

VENICE.

The screen of S. Mark has been so often depicted, that it has not been thought necessary to give a plate for its illustration; but it is a very fine example of an early Italian screen. Some writers have commonly described it as Byzantine, but it differs entirely from Greek screens, which are invariably solid, and entered by three doors; whereas that of S. Mark is open above the subase, and has only one pair of doors in the centre. It is a very remarkable work of the period, and decorated with several marble images above the entablature, executed by early Pisan sculptors. The images are of a much more recent date than the screen itself, which is one of the most ancient and best preserved examples of screens now remaining in Italy.

The church of Frairi, or Santa Maria Gloriosa, contains a very remarkable choir screen, which I have figured among the plates. It is composed of marble, and quite solid; the front is divided into compartments representing the prophets, boldly designed, and carved in bas-relief; at each end are the ambones for the Epistle and Gospel, with an angel for the book-bearer.

Beneath the corbels which support these ambones are the four Evangelists represented seated and writing the Gospels. The corbels themselves are beautifully wrought with cherubims and angels. The choir stalls within this screen are of elaborate Gothic-work, and ornamented with skilful inlay. Altogether, this church is another most striking example, out of multitudes of others, of the extreme fallacy and absurdity of the modern notion that Pointed architecture is unsuited to Italy and the south; and yet we hear this continually put forth in the most positive manner; and instead of men importing the grand ideas and spirit of those Italian artists who flourished in the mediæval era, we are inundated with the wild eccentricities of Bernini, or the more insipid productions of an even later school.

Not having visited Spain, I am not able to give any account of the church fittings from personal observation, but I have had an opportunity of inspecting several accurate drawings made on the spot, and from them it appears that huge screens of ornamental iron-work, reaching to a vast height, and elaborate in detail, are by no means uncommon. I have figured one on a small scale from the cathedral of Toledo, and I have little doubt that they greatly resemble the choir screens of St. Sernin at Toulouse, which I have given to a larger scale. This city partakes most strongly of a Spanish character, which strengthens my supposition regarding the similarity of the screen-work.

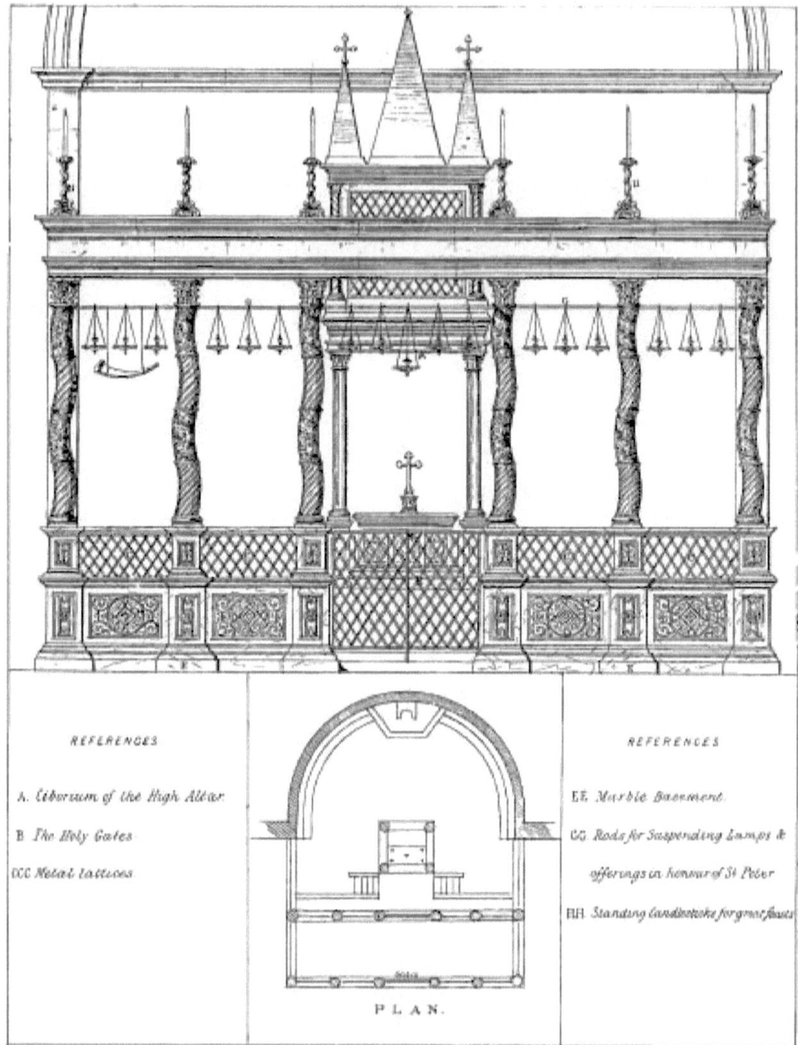

Elevation of Screen of Old St. Peters Church at Rome.
Plan of the Chancel of Ditto.

REFERENCES

A. *Ciborium of the High Altar.*

B. *The Holy Gates.*

CCC. *Metal lattices.*

REFERENCES

EE. *Marble Basement.*

GG. *Rods for Suspending Lamps & offerings in honour of St. Peter.*

HH. *Standing Candlesticks for great feasts.*

PLAN: Gates.

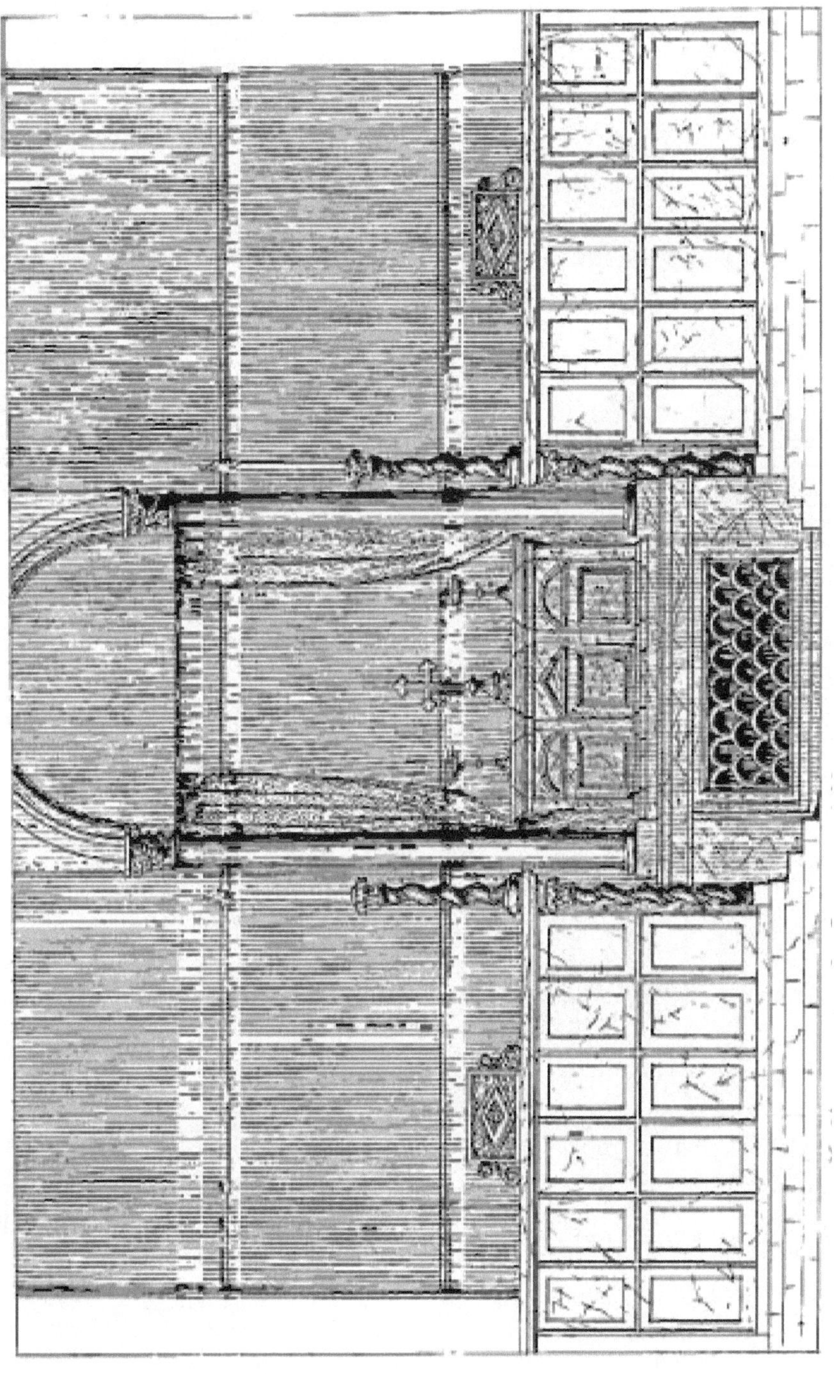

Marble Screen in the Basilica of SS Nerei and Achille, at Rome.

**Iron Screen from an ancient Painting at Sienna representing the life of
Pius the second, by Pinturicchio.**

Plate IV.

Marble Screen in the Church of the Frairi, Venice.

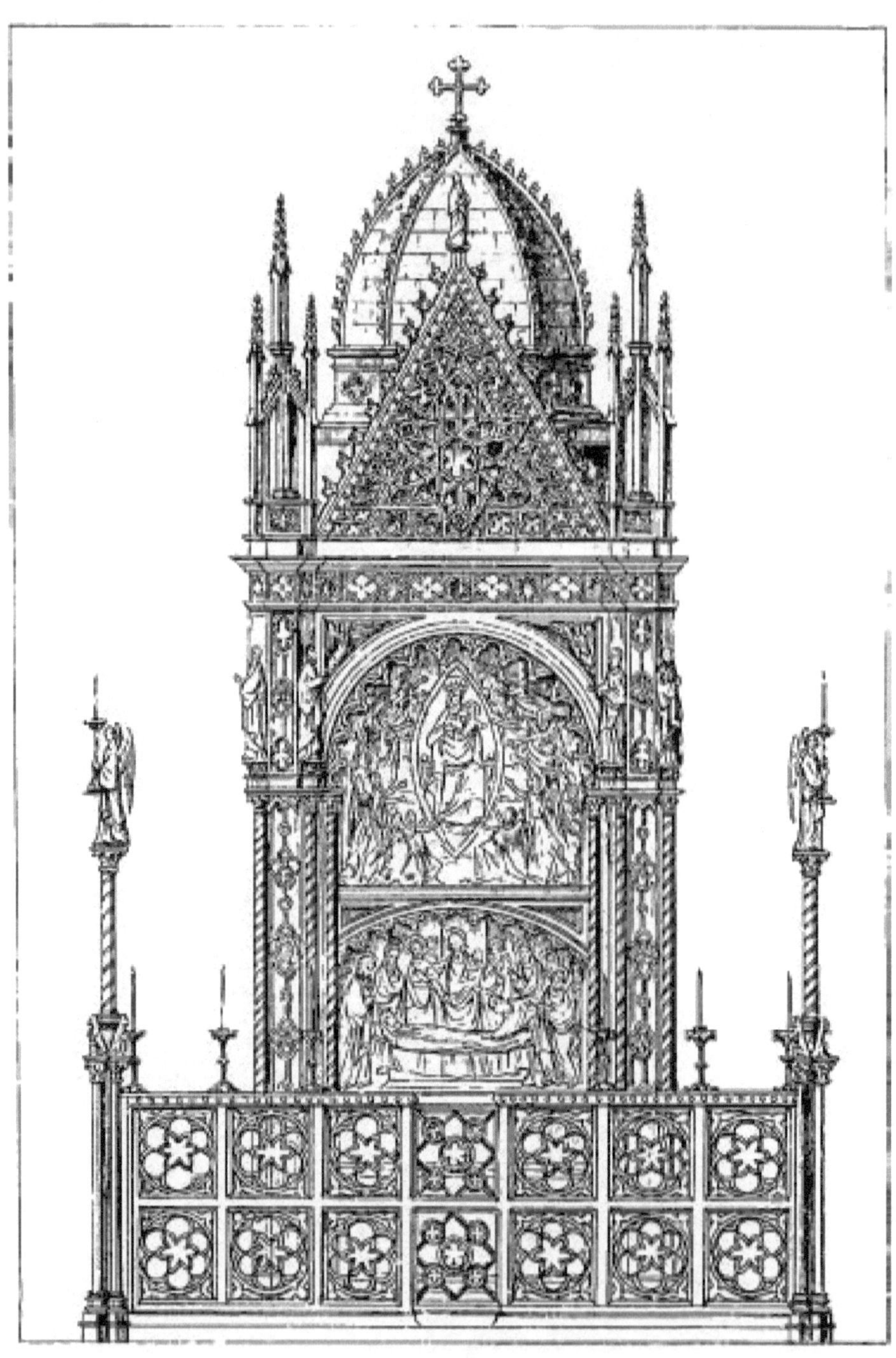

Detached Altar of St. Michele, Florence, with its Brass Screen.

ON SCREENS IN GERMANY AND FLANDERS.

SCREENS AT LUBECK.

The churches of this ancient city have preserved all their internal fittings as perfectly as those of Nuremberg, although the Catholic rites have ceased within them for nearly three centuries. The minutest ornaments remain intact, and but very trifling additions or alterations have been made in the original arrangement; accordingly, we find splendid examples of screens, which I have figured in the adjoining plates.

The first is in the Dom or cathedral. It originally consisted of three moulded arches, springing from slender quatrefoil shafts, supporting an open gallery. The choir was entered by two doors under the side arches, while an altar was erected in the centre compartment, and this arrangement is almost universal in the German screens, reversing the custom of France and England, of placing the entrance in the centre, with two lateral altars. This screen received a considerable quantity of enrichment in the way of imagery and tabernacle-work in the fifteenth century; the original arches are probably as old as the early part of the thirteenth. In Lutheran times, a clock has been added on the epistle side of this screen, which completely destroys its symmetry and appearance.

Two bays westward of this is a gigantic rood, on a beam, described under rood beams.

Each lateral chapel is enclosed by open screens, most artificially wrought in brass, and of great variety of design.

The next most important screen at Lubeck is in the Marienkirche. This screen consists of five bays, or compartments, with crocketed labels and images in the spandrels; the masonry is of the fourteenth century, but the upper panels, containing images and paintings, are not older than the fifteenth. As this was always a parochial church, the arches are all open, and filled with light brass-work. I examined them most carefully, and they evidently had been open according to the original design, nor were there any marks of altars ever standing under them as at *the cathedral*. The whole choir of this church, as well as the side chapels, are enclosed with light and beautiful brass screens, and a very elaborate screen of carved oak, surmounted by open bratishing, and basins for tapers, divides off the Lady chapel.

The Katherinen Kirche contains a most beautiful rood screen of very original design.

The church belonged formerly to religious, and the choir is raised some eighteen or twenty feet above the level of the church floor, supported by three ranges of vaulting resting on dwarf marble pillars, and forming a sort of above-ground crypt. Immediately over the front of these arches, rises the rood loft, fronted by carved panels, most beautifully painted with sacred images, and terminated in a very bold floriated bratishing of admirable execution; in the centre is the great rood, with the Evangelists in floriated quatrefoils, and the attendant images of our Blessed Lady and St. John, on octagonal pedestals. At the eastern end of the lower church is an enclosed choir, divided off by three light metal screens from the parishioners, so the religious and people had distinct altars, and were entirely separated in the same church—a most singular and beautiful arrangement.

The great Hospital is constructed like a church, with beds and chambers, open at top, under three vast roofs, covering a nave and aisles. The entrance to this is like a fore choir or antechapel, and dedicated for divine worship. It contains no less than five altars, three of which are under the arches of three screens, the stone-work of which is probably the oldest in Lubeck, and to which I should assign the date of the middle of the thirteenth century. The upper part of the loft, consisting of carved panels and paintings, is a work of the fifteenth century.

It is worthy of remark that, although the Lutheran religion has exclusively prevailed in this city for several centuries, many of the branches set up to burn tapers in front of the images in this and other churches bear the date of 1664, and even later.

St. James's church contains several wooden screens of a remarkably early date. They are certainly not later than the middle of the thirteenth century, and are most exquisitely carved with heads of saints, stringcourses, bratishing, images of doctors and evangelists in quatrefoils, and in style of art corresponding to the early work in Wells cathedral.

As this treatise is devoted to the subject of screens, I have confined my remarks to them, but I must add that I consider the churches of Lubeck to be the most interesting, as regards fittings and details, of any ecclesiastical buildings remaining in Europe. There are examples of metal-work, early painting, and wood-carving, of the thirteenth, fourteenth, and fifteenth centuries, and the finest monumental brass in the world, most probably by the same artist as produced the famous one at St. Alban's, but much larger and more elaborate.

MUNSTER.

The churches of this city having been completely sacked during the usurpation of the infamous John of Leyden, present few traces of the ancient furniture, and they are for the most part fitted up in the vilest possible taste. But the cathedral has by some good fortune retained its ancient screen and choir, which, with the exception of the high altar, remains in its original state. The screen is of stone, most richly carved, and composed of five bays, the centre one elevated over the others; under this is an altar, according to German custom, with two doors leading into the choir on each side. In the two external compartments there are two other altars, but these I conceive to be modern additions.

The eastern elevation of this screen, towards the choir, is most beautiful; there are three richly-canopied stalls at the back of the altar, and the loft, which is very spacious, is ascended by two openwork spiral staircases, of most elaborate design. The present rood is modern, and by no means commensurate in beauty with the screen; but there are evident marks of the former existence of a very large rood, partly supported by iron ties from the vaulting.

The lateral screens of the choir are solid, as is universally the case in cathedral churches; but those which enclose the side chapels are composed of brass and marble, and were erected in the *seventeenth century*, at the cost of the then bishop. Altogether, this choir is one of the most perfect in Germany, and, happily, restored for Catholic worship, without suffering any modernization.

BRUNSWICK.

Though a very unpromising name to Englishmen, who are accustomed to associate it with very modern times and places in their own country, is a most interesting ancient city, full of fine mediæval remains, and curious domestic architecture. The Dom (Lutheran) contains the remains of a rood screen and loft, with a central altar; but in a church now disused for worship, and of which I was unable to ascertain the name, a most elaborate screen, partly of stone, and partly of wood, is still standing uninjured; the style verges on the cinque-cento, but all the traditional forms and enrichments are preserved, and altogether it is a magnificent and imposing work.

The other churches have been much modernized in adapting them to Lutheran worship, which appears to vary in different places and countries to a very considerable extent; for while at Lubeck and Nuremberg the Catholic fittings remain intact, at Brunswick and other places they have nearly disappeared, and been replaced by modern abominations. Perhaps the preservation of these fine remains is principally owing to the want of funds in the cities whose commerce has decayed; they have not had the temporal means to spoil them. This is strikingly observable in remote parish churches in England, where no rates could be raised for their repairs, for they are usually in a very perfect state; while in large and populous towns, the churchwardens have had so much to expend, that they are completely gutted and ruined.

HILDESHEIM.

The cathedral, though it has suffered most severely from extensive alterations in the seventeenth century, has still preserved a most curious stone rood loft, debased in style, but still carrying out the principles of the old traditions. It was approached by two flights of steps, the choir being elevated over a crypt, which gives it a most imposing appearance. On the top of the first platform is an altar, and immediately over it a stone pulpit, with a brass lectern, on the left side, in the form of an eagle, doubtless for the deacon to sing the holy Gospel to the people. On either side of this are doors, with gates of open metal-work; above are five arched canopies, which contain sculptures in alto-relief, representing the sacrifice of Abraham;

bearing the cross; entombment of our Lord; Jonas and the whale; and under the foot of the rood, in the centre, Moses setting up the brazen serpent in the wilderness; an appropriate type of the great reality, our Lord lifted up on the cross, or rood, which is, as usual, sculptured with the attendant images of St. John and the Blessed Virgin. There are two Byzantine coronæ for lights still suspended in this church, and many of the details of the choir, crypt, &c. are exceedingly interesting.

BREMEN.

This cathedral has been much modernized by the Lutherans, but the ancient rood loft, though removed from its original position, is still standing in the church, as a sort of gallery. The sculpture is of a very superior description, and it may be ascribed to the early or middle part of the fifteenth century. In the centre part of the aisle are some exceedingly curious fragments of stall-work, as old as the thirteenth century, which doubtless formed a portion of the original choir fittings. They are very remarkable in design and execution, being cut out of huge oak planks, several inches thick, and, though somewhat rude, have a fine, bold, and severe character.

BASLE.

This cathedral, now used for Lutheran worship, has a very fine close screen, with the remains of a central altar, and two side doorways.

FRIEDBERG AND GELNHAUSEN.

Have the same arrangement, as may be seen by the plates.

MARBURG.

The screen is a decorated wall, entirely shutting off the choir, with an altar in the centre. See plate.

HALBERSTADT.

Has a fine rood loft, of the end of the fifteenth, or beginning of the sixteenth century.

ULM.

The central altar, surmounted with screen and canopy-work, is still remaining; but the connecting work between it and the stalls has been removed, probably about the middle of the last century, and an iron railing substituted. This church, which is one of the finest in Germany for its elevation and interesting details, is now used for the Lutheran worship, but, with the exception of this screen, the original fittings remain perfect.

S. LAWRENCE CHURCH, NUREMBERG.

Here the great rood is supported by an arched beam, over the entrance of the choir, and as it is some years since I visited this church, I am not prepared to state positively if this is the ancient arrangement; but as I have never seen a corresponding example in a Pointed church where the fittings are coeval with the date of the edifice, I should greatly doubt it; especially as it is most certain that this portion of the building has undergone considerable alterations in adapting it to the Lutheran rites.

The ancient arrangement of these German screens, with the central altar and side doors, is often depicted in pictures by the early masters. I may mention one remarkable instance at the Gallery of the Academy, Antwerp. The background of a small picture of our Blessed Lady represents the interior of a church. The screen is depicted as of grey marble, supported on porphyry pillars. The holy doors, of perforated brass-work, are closed, and the whole is surmounted by a rood and accompanying images. The arms of the cross are supported by elaborate metal chains, descending from the vaulting.

THE GREAT CHURCH AT OBERWESEL.

Has one of the most perfect, as well as the most beautiful screens in Germany (see plate); but in its arrangement it resembles the French, rather than the German types, as the entrance to the choir is in the centre, and there are two side altars in the vaulted space under the loft. The details of this screen are most beautifully wrought, and the mouldings are of the purest form. This church was served by religious, and the screen is therefore solid, and panelled, to correspond with the division of the pillars. The screen is not the only interesting object in this church. The stalls are finely wrought, and the high altar is surmounted by a splendid triptych, richly painted and gilt. The sacristy remains in the original state; there are several incised slabs and mural paintings, and altogether it is a church of very great interest.

HAARLEM.

The Dutch churches have, for the most part, been completely gutted of their ancient Catholic fittings, but S. Bavon, at Haarlem, is a fortunate exception. It has preserved the brazen screens of its choir; they are of wrought work, exceedingly open, and very similar in design and execution to those at Lubeck. There can be no doubt that all the churches were provided originally with similar screen-work, the traces of which may be frequently discerned in the piers and pillars. I have been informed of some brass screens yet remaining in the more northern part of Holland; but not having personal knowledge of them, I can give no description of their dates or design. There is, however, quite sufficient to establish the great fact, that in Catholic times the Dutch churches were in no way inferior in this respect, but that screens were as usual in them as in other parts of Christendom.[11]

The finest example of a Pointed screen remaining in Belgium is at Louvain; but even this has been sadly modernized, and its use and symbolical signification both destroyed. It consists at present of three open arches, through which people can pass into the choir. Within the memory of many persons yet living, the side

[11] I have been informed, from good authority, that one of the churches in Amsterdam has preserved its brass screen-work, but I am not able to supply the name.

arches were filled by two altars and reredoses, and the centre one closed by two gates of open metal-work. The removal of this beautiful and essential furniture for the screen was coeval with the destruction of the sedilia, the demolition of the ancient high altar, and the substitution of a Pagan design in marble, and a variety of other enormities, by which the whole character and ecclesiastical arrangement of the choir was destroyed; and what is most lamentable, all this was brought to pass by those very ecclesiastical authorities who ought to have been foremost in preserving the ancient traditions.

But to return. The upper part of the screen and rood loft is still, happily, perfect, and is surmounted by the original rood, with its attendant images. The details of the cross are admirably executed, and the whole effect is most striking and devotional. The cross is gilt, and relieved in colour; the images are also painted. The arms of the cross are supported by wrought-iron chains, fixed to the stonework of the great arch, on the rood loft. The three staples to sustain these chains may yet be discerned in most of the Belgian churches, and point out the ancient position of the rood, which modern innovation has removed.

DIXMUDE.

Has a very late florid screen and rood loft. It is divided like that of Louvain, into three compartments. The altars, which, however, have been much modernized, are still remaining. The decorations, as well as the reredoses, are of the seventeenth century. The loft is surmounted by a rood.

AERSCOT.

The rood loft in this church is of the same date as that of Dixmude, and most probably designed by the same artist; the side altars here are also remaining, but covered with decorations of the seventeenth century, in very bad taste.

The rood, crucifix, Blessed Virgin, and St. John are still remaining.

LOUVAIN.

S. Gertrude.—The screen was much injured by alteration in the seventeenth century; but, though modernized, it retained a great deal of its original character, till the monstrous idea was conceived, about three years ago, of suppressing the return stalls, and throwing open the whole choir. This has been very lately carried into execution, and the church has suffered most materially, not only in its church arrangements, but in the general effect of the building.

The Dominican church had a fine rood and screen, of which there are still some remains, though greatly injured by the widening of the choir entrance.

TOURNAI.

A huge rood screen of black and white marble, erected in the seventeenth century, surmounted by a crucifix, and decorated with sculptures. Although erected at a very debased period, it still retains all the old traditional arrangements.

BRUGES.

S. Salvator's.—A black and white marble screen and loft of the seventeenth century. It is divided into three arched compartments, but without altars; the side spaces are filled with open brass-work, and the choir gates, or holy doors, are of the same material.[12]

Notre Dame.—A screen of a very similar description, only of a plainer character. It is remarkable for having the altar erected in the centre of the loft, out of which grows the great rood, supporting the crucifix.

S. Giles's church has a very curious screen of the seventeenth century, exceedingly rich in carving, and supporting a rood loft. It is designed in perfect conformity to the ancient traditions, although the detail is necessarily of a debased period.

THE CHURCH OF HAL, NEAR BRUSSELS.

Must have had a very fine rood loft originally, but being a place of pilgrimage, it became most unfortunately very rich from offerings, which were employed (with the best possible intention) to destroy the ancient furniture of the church; the great rood itself, elaborately carved, hangs up on the south side of the great tower, and is a fine specimen of what the beauty of the loft must have been in the old time.

ANTWERP.

This great cathedral was completely sacked by the Calvinists, in the latter part of the sixteenth century, previous to which its fittings were in perfect unison with the edifice. But, unfortunately, when it was restored to Catholic worship, the spirit of Paganism had entered into the arts, and the new furniture exhibited all the marks of debasement. However, the old traditions still ruled the mind as regarded principles, and it will be seen, by reference to the plate, that the screens were conceived in the old spirit; and although the introduction of altars against the nave pillars was a great and distressing innovation, yet they were still protected by elevated screen-work, and not left open for profanation. There is a most striking correspondence between this screen-work and that round the altar of S. Michele, at Florence. The whole of these fittings have disappeared, partly during the occupation of the French, and partly by injudicious repairs. The choir is now being lined with stalls, some of the details of which are deserving of great commendation, but they have been designed in utter contradiction to ecclesiastical tradition. If this is to be made a cathedral church, the choir should be enclosed; but if it is to serve a parochial purpose, instead of the lofty canopies, and solid back, the choir should have been enclosed with open metal screens, like those at Lubeck, and an open

[12] The screen across the Bootmakers' Chapel, in the north transept of this church, is of a great antiquity, probably of the middle of the fourteenth century. It is executed entirely in oak, most beautifully carved; and skilfully framed in the rails of the doors are bas-reliefs of angels bearing the cognizance of the confraternity of bootmakers, at whose cost this chapel was erected and founded. There are other oak screens in the south transept of a later date, fifteenth century, and the choir and lateral chapels are all arched, with marble screens, filled with perforated brass-work.

rood loft across the choir; at present it is neither one thing nor the other. The whole entrance of the choir is open to the public, who crowd up to the high altar, and the stalls are filled with the first comers; the whole arrangement is disgraceful, unecclesiastical, and irregular, and loudly calls for reform. Frequented as this church is by such masses of people, the screen should certainly be an open one, and the back, above the stalls, should correspond. There are two enormous canopies, over nothing, that stand against the pillars; at first I imagined they indicated the seat of some dean or dignitary, but I soon found they projected only over a vacant space, by which the stalls were ascended, and were simply placed there as a vehicle for exhibiting a great assemblage of pinnacles and buttresses, and expending a sum of money unhappily, that would have half built the rood loft. The authority from which I have taken the representation of the old screen, &c., is a picture by Peter Neefs, preserved at Bicton, the seat of Lady Rolle.

All the churches in Antwerp have been wofully modernized; but there is something like a screen at S. James's: two huge masses of marble wall, projecting from each of the great pillars, at the entrance of the choir. It is a work of the seventeenth century, heavy, and ill-contrived; and for a parochial church, most unsuitable.

GHENT.

The cathedral of S. Bavon has two projections of a similar description, leaving the space open in the centre for an entrance to the choir. These form lofts at top, and are ascended by staircases. On Sundays and festivals, I regret to add, they are filled with *fiddlers*! Were they joined at top, this would form a regular rood loft, but as it stands at present, it is a most anomalous pile of marble-work, effectually shutting out half the choir, without any attempt at beauty or symbolism.

The old Dominican church has a remarkable screen of the seventeenth century; it is overloaded with sculpture and ornament of a very bad period; but it has a rood and loft, and it separates the choir from the nave of the church, which, like the usual Dominican churches, consists of a long parallelogram, with side chapels, gained out of the projection of the buttresses. The building itself is of the fine, severe Pointed style that prevailed in the fourteenth century; but all the fittings, erected probably at the same time as the screen, are of very debased character. It may be proper to remark that all the side chapels of the great Belgian churches are enclosed by marble screens, intermixed with perforated brass-work. These are mostly the work of the early part of the seventeenth century, and no doubt replaced the more ancient oak and metal screens that were mutilated or destroyed by the Calvinists in the devastating religious wars of the Low Countries. They are an existing proof that the traditional principles of enclosure and reverence outlived the change of style of architecture; for, although all these are of debased Italian design, they are constructed principally on the old arrangement, and are usually surmounted by standards for tapers.

The custom of screening off these side chapels was universal. We find them in Italy at a very early period (see Bologna), and many beautiful pointed examples, both in wood and stone, exist in Germany, France, and England; they are subsequently found of every date and style. In the eighteenth century they were usually constructed with elaborate wrought-iron-work, and in our time of a simple form in the same material; but the principle still remains in every part of Christendom, excepting some of the most modern Italian churches, where all tradition seems to have been lost, or abandoned by their artists and architects.

This account of screens in Germany and Flanders is necessarily very incomplete; but it is sufficient to illustrate the intention of the work, and anything like a complete list would be both too voluminous and tedious to the reader.

Chancel screens appear to be very general in the old timber churches of Norway, and I have figured one in the church of Urnes, near Bergen, which is exceedingly interesting; and though it is by no means easy to affix dates to these rude productions, there is every reason to suppose this to be a work of considerable antiquity. This church is now used for Lutheran worship, but, like every ancient edifice erected for Catholic rites, it bears indelible evidence of the enclosure of the chancel and the erection of the rood.

Rood Screen of the Marienkirche, Lubeck.

Rood Loft, Cathedral, Munster.

Screen in the Dom Kirke, Lubeck.

Screen and Rood Loft, Hospital, Lubeck.

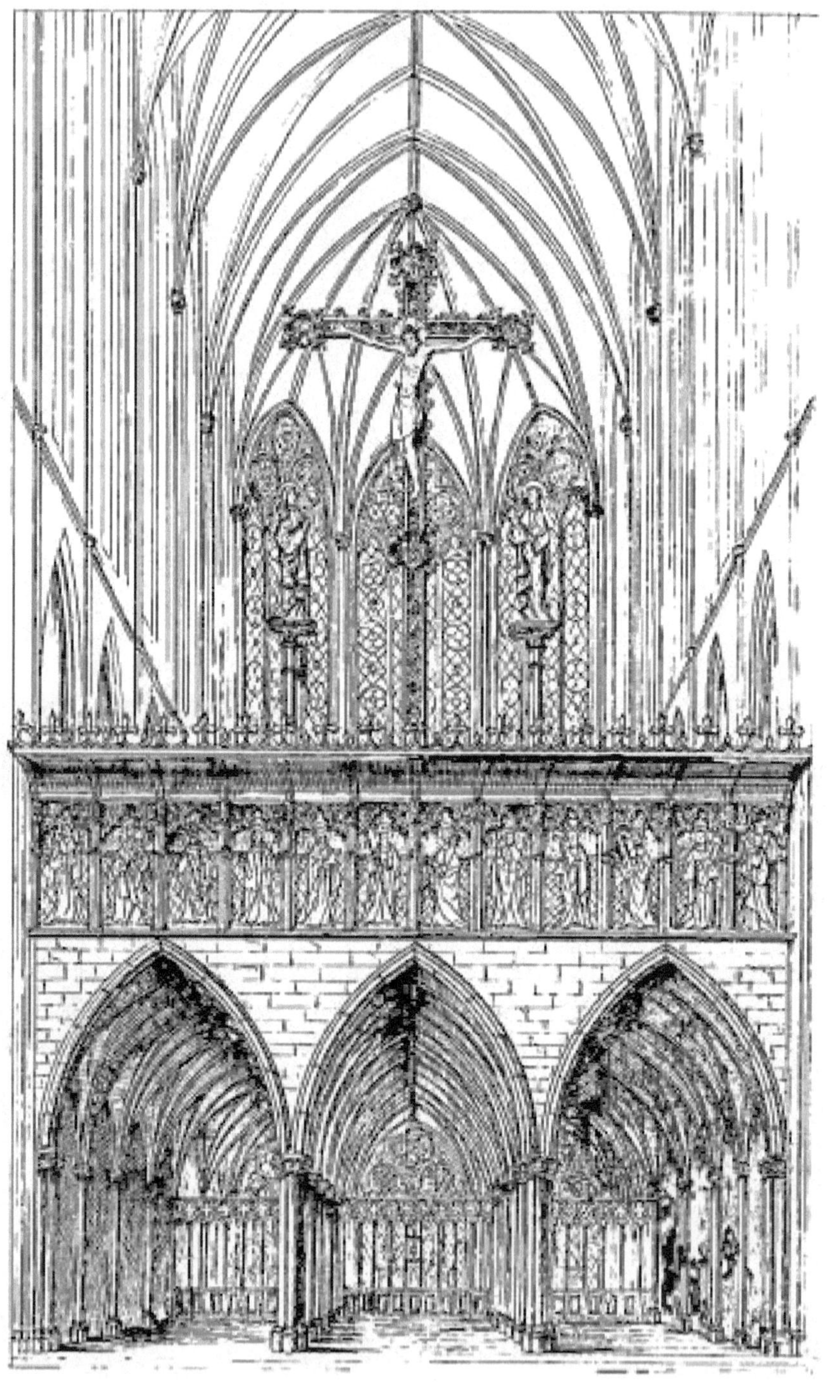

Rood Loft St. Katherine's Church, Lubeck.

Screen and rood Loft Dom, Hildesheim.

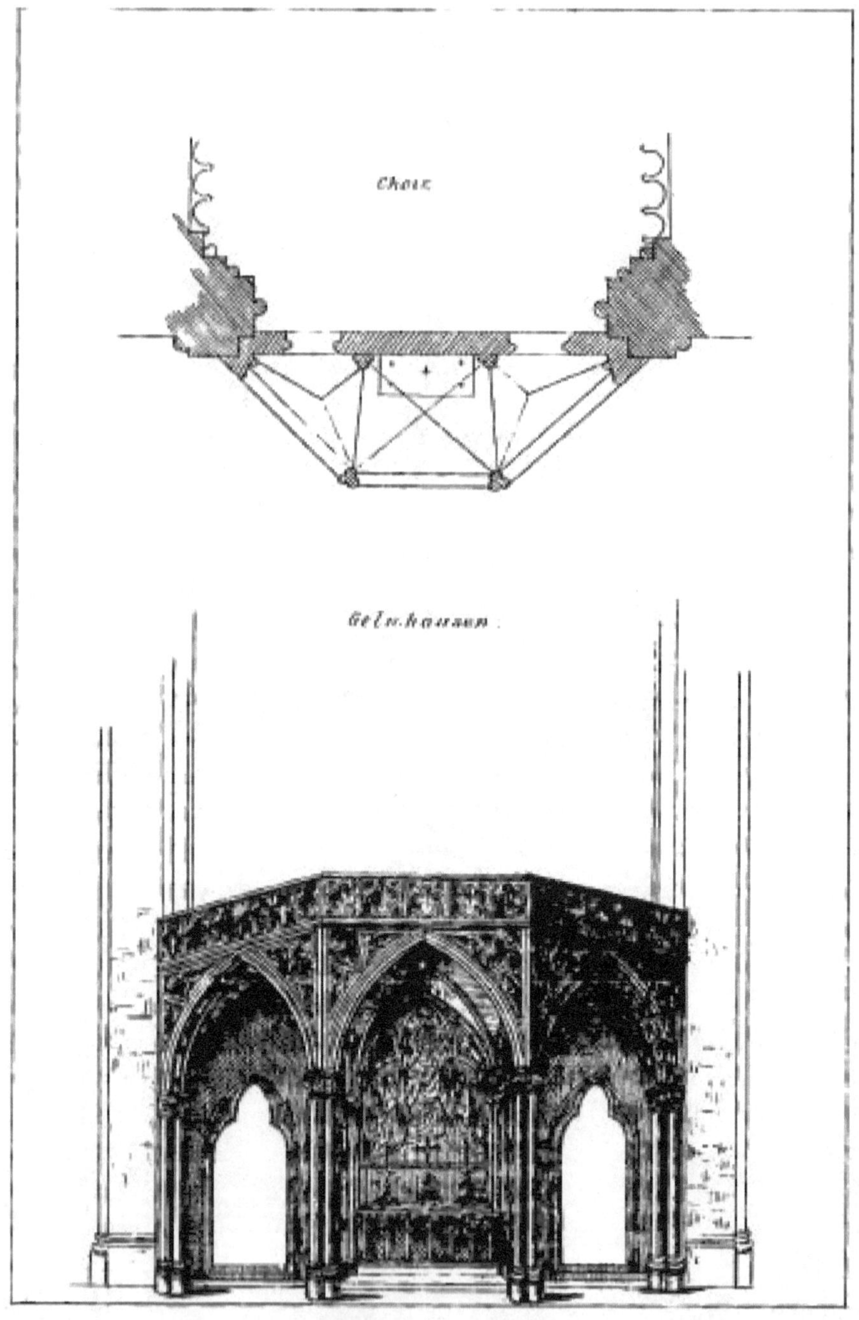

Choir; Gelnhausen.

Screen at Glenhausen.

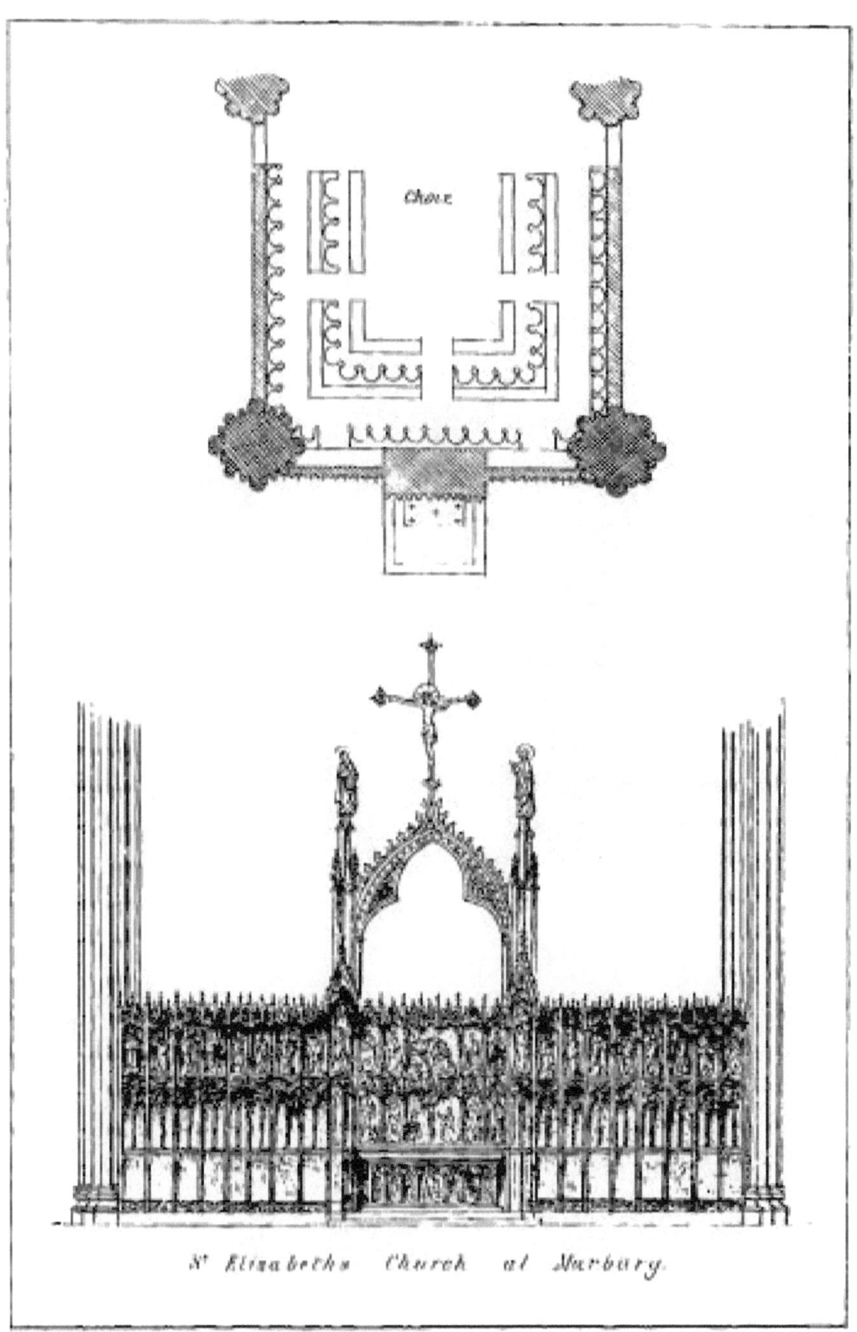

Choir.

St. Elisabeth's Church at Marburg.

Screen at Oberwesel.

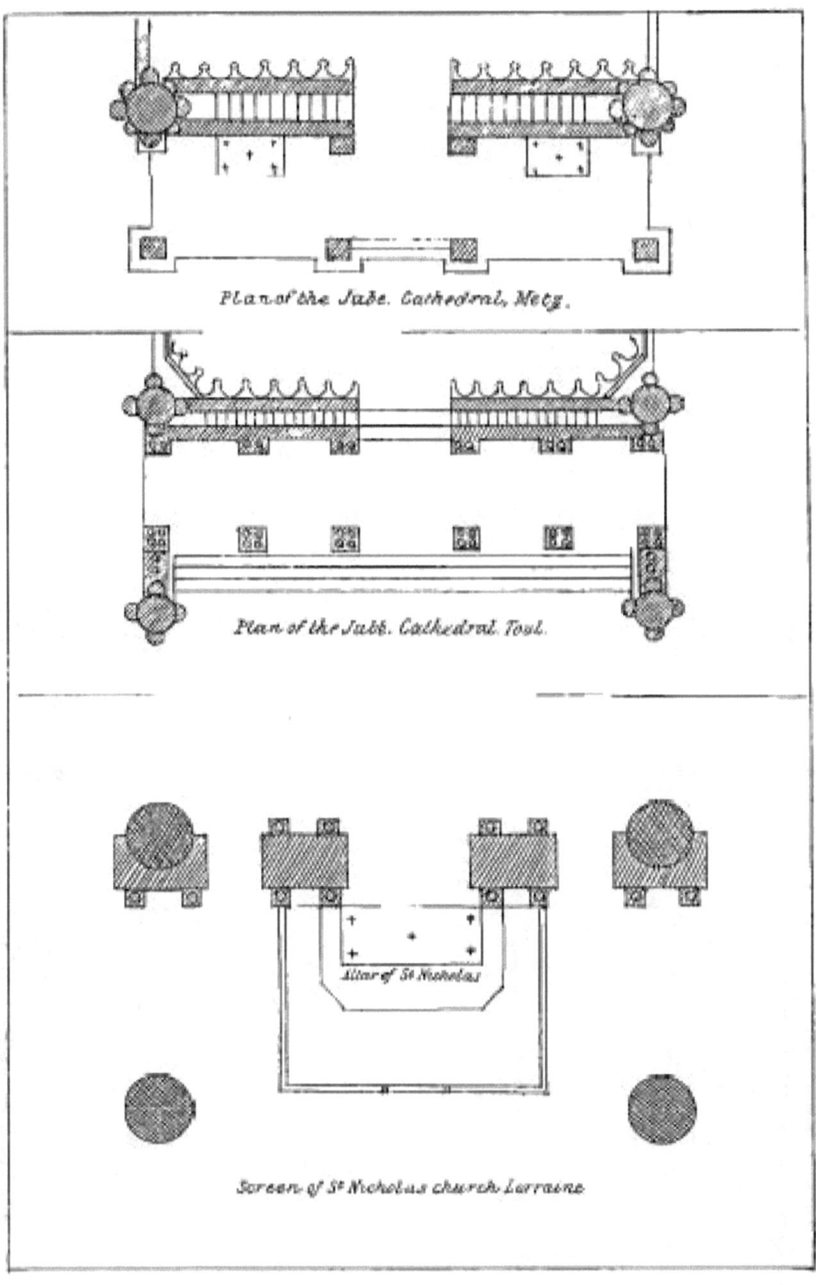

Plan of the Jubé. Cathedral, Metz.
Plan of the Jubé. Cathedral, Toul.
Screen of St. Nicholas church, Lorraine.

The Rood Screen, Cathedral, Antwerp. 17 Century.

From an Old Picture by Peter Neefs.

One of the Altars, erected against the Nave Pillars, with its Brass Screen work.

From an Old Picture by Peter Neefs.

ON SCREENS IN FRANCE.

CATHEDRAL OF AMIENS.

Previous to the year 1755, the choir of Amiens cathedral had retained its ancient and magnificent fittings,—altar, sedilia, jubé, all were perfect; but at that fatal period, Mons. de la Mothe, a pious and well-intentioned bishop, but a man of execrable taste, and devoid of all feeling for true ecclesiastical architecture, conceived the unfortunate project of modernizing this glorious choir: and, at an enormous expense, the ancient works were demolished, to be replaced by the incongruous masses of marble clouding and meretricious decorations that so wofully disfigure this noble church. Then was it, and *not till then*, that the great jubé was removed, that most wonderful book of stone, as Mons. Duval most aptly terms it, in which the people had, for so many centuries, beheld a lively representation of the life and sufferings of our Lord. At the same time, eight of the unrivalled stalls were hewn down to widen the choir gates; and the remainder of this matchless work of Arnould Boulen were only suffered to remain on account of the immense cost of replacing them by modern work.

These barbarous innovations were strongly opposed by many members of the chapter, but the influence of M. de la Mothe prevailed, to the irreparable loss of this mighty fabric.

It is worthy of remark that a pastoral letter of M. de Sebatier, the predecessor of M. de la Mothe in the see of Amiens, is still preserved, in which that prelate actually recommends the destruction and removal of ancient imagery and furniture from the churches in his diocese, as incompatible with *simplicity* and *cleanliness*! Such were the ideas of the men under whom the great churches of France were mutilated and disfigured.

"Nous avons été surpris de voir que dans les églises où l'on avait fait des dépenses considérables et de nouvelles décorations, on y eut étalé les mauvais restes des tabernacles, des figures mutilées, et des autres vieux ornements, dans d'autres endroits de l'église, où ils ne sont pas moins difformes que dans l'endroit dont on les a tirés, et qui bien loin de servir d'ornement, ne servent qu'à amasser de la poussière, et y faire un nouvel embarras. Nous aurions donc souhaité que les figures mutilées eussent été enterrées secrètement dans la cimetière, et les vieux ornements, ou de bois ou de pierre, vendus, s'ils en valaient la peine, au profit de la fabrique, plutôt que de rester dans cet état. C'est aussi ce que nous espérons qu'on fera dans la suite pour éviter la confusion qu'un amas inutile de ces vieux restes a coutume de causer dans les églises dont la propreté et la simplicité doivent faire le principal ornement."

ABBAYE DE S. BERTIN, S. OMERS.

The Abbé de Condite is mentioned in the cartulary of S. Berlin as having erected in 1402 a jubé or doxale of wood, decorated with many images in copper, gilt. This jubé was replaced by one of black and white marble, commenced in the year 1621, and completed in 1626.

The entrance to the choir was closed by brass gates of open design, and the whole was surmounted by a great crucifix suspended from the vaulting, with the accompanying images of St. Mary and St. John. This cross was made by Abbot Simon II. in the twelfth century, and was doubtless the same that belonged to the ancient jubé. This grand church was desecrated and ruined in the great revolution, and *totally demolished under the Restoration!*

S. QUENTIN.

The choir of this church was enclosed by sculptures representing the life of the patron saint, under canopies similar to those at Amiens cathedral, with a jubé of the same character. Both destroyed at the revolution in 1790.

CATHEDRAL OF LYONS.[13]

The old jubé was demolished by the Huguenots in 1562, and rebuilt by the canons in 1585, as was proved by the following inscription, cut on a marble slab:—

QUOD . BELL . CIVIL LICENTIA.
FOEDE . DISIECTUM FUERAT
D.O.M. PROPITIO . CAN . ET COM.
LUG REST . CC . AN . MD.LXXXV.

This screen was entirely demolished in the revolution of 1790.—Thiers's Dissertation sur les Jubés.

CATHEDRAL OF ORLEANS.

A jubé of marble, designed by J. Hardouin Mansard, was erected in 1690, and destroyed, as well as the choir stalls, in the great revolution.

ABBEY OF S. DENIS, NEAR PARIS.

Dom Michel Felibien, a Benedictine monk of the Maurist congregation, thus describes a screen erecting at St. Denis in his time: "They are now working at the erection of a screen of iron-work, of the Ionic order, with pilasters terminating in caryatides; the centre door will be surmounted by a cross, covered with plates of gold, enriched with ornaments and precious stones, the workmanship of which is traditionally ascribed to S. Eligius."—Histoire de l'Abbaye Royale de S. Denis;

[13] De Moleon mentions in his voyage that three silver crosses, each holding three tapers, were suspended in the rood loft, under standing candlesticks; he also describes the jubé as being built of marble, and of what was considered in his time a fine design.

Paris, 1706, p. 533.

From this description it is evident that this screen, with the exception of the cross, must have been of wretched design; still there is all the principle of the olden arrangement; and in the plan of the church figured in the same work, the two staircases leading up to the ambones for the Epistle and Gospel are distinctly marked. This screen, which replaced the ancient jubé, probably erected in the time of Abbot Suger, was entirely demolished in 1792.

NOTRE DAME DE MANTES.

"The jubé, separating the choir from the nave, was of wrought stone, with open arches, supported by pillars. On each side of the entrance were chapels and altars; that on the left hand dedicated to the Blessed Virgin, with a (*retable*) reredos, decorated with small bas-reliefs of our Lord's passion, painted and gilt, similar in style to that behind the high altar of the church. In the gallery of the jubé (rood loft), on an elevation of several steps, was an image of St. John, supporting a desk from whence the Gospel was chanted. Above this jubé was a large cross of wood, gilt and painted, and covered with fleur-de-lis, which extended nearly the width of the church, having an image of our Lord crucified, and on either side two cherubim, with wings of gold, and beyond these, images of the Blessed Virgin and St. John in mantles, covered with fleur-de-lis, with borders of inscriptions. This was demolished in 1788, at the same time that the chapter removed the splendid ancient altar, with its brass pillars and ciborium, and replaced it by a miserable design, described (*à la Romaine*). Within three years after this destruction the church was in the hands of revolutionists, the clergy expelled, and the new-fashioned altar, &c. reduced to a heap of fragments."—See Antiquités Nationales, par Aubin Louis Millin: Paris, l'an second de la liberté, 1791.

ABBAYE DE FONTENELLE, OR S. WANDRILLE.

"The original jubé was destroyed by the fall of the great central tower, on the night of the 21st of December, 1631. A new screen was commenced in 1670, and completed in 1672, by Emmanuel Boynet, architect. It was supported by four marble pillars, with two altars on each side the choir door."—Essai sur l'Abbaye de Fontenelle, par E. Hyacinthe Langlois: Paris, 1827.

CONVENTUAL CHURCH OF THE GRANDS AUGUSTINES, PARIS.

"The jubé, which separates the choir from the nave, is of a very ordinary design, and built in the year 1665. It is supported by ten Corinthian pillars, in Dorian marble, between the clusters of which are two altars, one dedicated to the Blessed Virgin, the other to S. Nicholas of Tolentino."—Antiquités Nationales, par Aubin Louis Millin: Paris, l'an second de la liberté, 1791, page 57, vol. iii.

CHURCH OF THE MATHURINS, PARIS.

"The choir is separated from the nave by six Ionic columns of Flemish marble, supporting an entablature of stone, supporting a large image of our Lord crucified, and several images of angels bearing emblems of the passion: the spaces between the pillars are filled with rich iron-work. The whole was completed about 1640."— Ibid. vol. iii. p. 14.

RHEIMS.

The rood loft was constructed in 1420; it was twenty-nine feet in height, forty-two wide, and thirteen deep, ascended by two staircases of open tracery, and provided, as usual, with two altars. This exquisite monument of mediæval art, covered with imagery and sculpture, was demolished in 1747, to be replaced by a heavy and lofty iron railing, in the Rococo style of that debased period.

Mons. de Jolimont, in his notice on Rheims cathedral, writes in the following manner on this destruction: "Le chœur était anciennement entouré d'une clôture en pierre, et l'entrée fermée par un magnifique jubé, monument curieux du quinzième siècle, orné d'autels, de statues, de colonnes, d'escaliers en spirale, et de sculptures les plus délicates; il fut détruit, comme tant d'autres, à une époque où le mauvais goût faisait une guerre à outrance au *Gothique*, ou pour satisfaire la vanité des gens opulens qui croyaient bien mériter de la posterité, en substituant à grands frais, à ces respectables antiquités, de prétendus embellissemens de mode, que les motifs les plus puériles semblaient rendre nécessaires; on doit déplorer, dans l'église de Reims, plus d'un exemple de cette espèce d'attentat officieux."— Chapuy, Cathédrales Françaises.

S. NICAISE, RHEIMS.

The jubé of this church was erected in 1507, and its sculptured front represented the history of the Old Testament from Noah to Daniel. It was utterly destroyed at the great revolution.

S. GATIEN, TOURS.

When De Moleon wrote his Voyage Liturgique, the choir of this church was enclosed with brass screens, seven feet high, and the great rood loft was standing perfect. His book was printed in 1757.

THE CHURCH OF SOUVIGNY, IN THE BOURBONNAIS.

Has still preserved a most elegant choir screen. It is divided by slender stone mullions into compartments, filled with light and elegant tracery, surmounted by crocketed canopy-work, terminated by bratishing. It is a work of the fifteenth century, and greatly resembles the English screens of the same period, both in design and detail.

ABBAYE DE S. OUEN, ROUEN.

The splendid screen and rood loft that once decorated this most glorious church is figured in Dom Pomeraye's history of this famous abbey.

It consisted of three divisions of double arches, supported by clusters of pinnacles and niches; the two centre ones were carried up higher than the others, and were terminated by two images, of St. John and the Blessed Virgin; a crocketed arch, enriched with tracery cusps, was carried up between these pinnacles, and supported the great crucifix; under this arch was an image of our Lady of Pity. The choir gates were of pierced-work in brass, and on either side two altars, surmounted by many images of saints in tabernacles. The loft was ascended by two spiral staircases, of most ingenious construction, and enriched with tracery, panels, and sculpture. Over the engraving of this screen is the following significant inscription, in French:

"Jubé of the church of S. Ouen: Erected in the year of our Lord 1462, by the Cardinal D'Estouteville; ruined by the heretics in 1562; and restored in 1656, by Dom Guillaume Cotterel, grand prior of the abbey."

This screen was finally demolished by the infidel revolutionists of 1790, who turned the church into a smith's workshop, and who found that the screen impeded the *progress of their waggons through the choir*!

The following notice of the screen occurs in the text:

"It was through the liberality of Cardinal D'Estouteville that the jubé was erected, which is one of the most beautiful and delicately-worked screens in existence. It was universally admired, and would still command the same admiration, had it not so severely suffered from the fury of the heretics. It is so skilfully placed, that neither the appearance of the transept or the choir are the least injured. It was formerly covered with admirable images and carvings, but these miserable sectaries, who could not endure the sight of this fine work, which, although almost new, was older than their false religion, attacked it with their accustomed fury, and completely defaced the images of holy personages with which it was covered, together with its exquisite details and ornaments. At the same time the Calvinists pulled down and carried off all the lateral absidal screens of the choir, which were of solid brass, most curiously wrought."—See Histoire de l'Abbaye Royale de S. Ouen, de Rouen, par un religieux Bénédictin de la Congrégation de S. Maur: Rouen, 1662; pp. 192 and 198.[14]

[14] *Extrait de l'Histoire de S. Ouen, de Rouen.*

Ce fut par sa magnificence que l'on bastit le jubé, qui étoit une des plus belles et des plus delicates pièces que l'on eust pû voir, et que l'on admireroit encore aujourd'huy, si depuis il n'auoit ressenty les effets de la rage des hérétiques. Il est placé avec tant d'adresse, que n'y la croisée n'y le chœur n'en sont aucunement incommodez. Il étoit enrichy d'excellentes figures et de quantité de rares embellissemens qui étoient sortis de la main d'un très habile ouvrier. Mais ces malheureux, ne pouvant souffrir ce bel ouvrage, qui bien que quasi tout neuf, ne laissoit pas d'estre beaucoup plus ancien que leur fausse religion, et de leur en reprocher la nouveauté, le ruinerent avec leur fureur accoûtumée, et jetterent par terre toutes les saintes images et tous les autres ornemens, qui étoient autant de chefs-d'œuvres de sculpture. Mais ce ne fut pas là la plus grande perte qu'ils causèrent à cette Abbaye, ainsi que nous dirons. Les armes de ce magnifique cardinal qui étoient sous le jubé, c'est à dire, dessus la porte par où l'on entre de la nef dans le chœur, furent abatues et détruites dans ce mesme pillage; et ci celles qui sont au haut d'une vitre du costé de la croisée, par où l'on descend dans le cloistre, n'eussent esté hors de la prise de ces furieux, elles eussent aussi

ROUEN CATHEDRAL.

Langlois, Notice sur l'Incendie de la Cathédrale de Rouen:—

"1467. The stalls of the choir erected. The ancient jubé was probably built at the same time.

"1526. An open screen-work of brass, most artificially wrought, set up round the sides of choir, at the cost of the Cardinal D'Amboise.

"1562. Pillage of the cathedral by the Calvinists, the jubé defaced, and the brass screens carried off and melted.

"1639. A new altar, dedicated to the Blessed Virgin, was erected under the screen, in consequence of a vow made during a pestilence.

"1642. A new altar, dedicated in honour of S. Cecily, erected under the screen.

"1777. The chapter erect a new screen (consisting of eight marble pillars, of the Ionic order, surmounted by an entablature and open balustrade. In the centre a large crucifix, and two marble altars, with images on either side of the choir gates)."

This screen is still standing, and although of execrable design, and most incongruous with the noble church in which it has been erected, it is still a proof that, at the end of the eighteenth century, a screen and rood loft was considered necessary by the clergy of this cathedral, and being entirely of white marble, its cost was far greater than that for which a splendid screen in perfect character with the church could have been constructed.

CATHEDRAL OF AUXERRE.

"The choir is vast, and was formerly enclosed by a jubé, but which was demolished by the Calvinists in the latter part of the sixteenth century."—Vues Pittoresques de la Cathédrale d'Auxerre, par Chapuy: Paris, 1828; p. 9.

The choir is at present enclosed by an iron railing, about fourteen feet high; an arch of scroll-work is carried up over the centre gates, and supports a cross.—A. W. P.

CATHEDRAL OF CHARTRES.

The ancient jubé was sixty-six feet long, and twelve feet nine inches wide. It was divided into seven compartments by slender shafts, and richly decorated with sculpture, foliage, and pinnacles; it was ascended by two staircases, approached from either side of the choir door.

This screen was only demolished in 1772, and then not with a view of throwing open the choir, but of substituting a wretched design of debased Italian, which I have figured in this work. It is worthy of remark, that coeval with this alteration, the following atrocities were perpetrated: the ancient altar, erected in 1520, with its pillars of brass, supporting curtains, and surmounted by angels bearing cancouru la mesme fortune.

dlesticks, and the whole terminated by a venerable image of our Blessed Lady in silver, was removed to make room for the Pagan sarcophagus which serves for the present altar. The clustered shafts and foliage capitals of the choir pillars were encased with marble veneers, and converted into heavy square piers and pilasters of Italian design, and the ancient stalls, with their fine canopies, were demolished.

Monsieur Louis, the architect of the Duc d'Orleans, conducted these lamentable alterations, which, as might be expected, were rapidly succeeded by the still more destructive power of the revolution. Vide Vues de la Cathédrale de Chartres, par Chapuy, pp. 22 and 23.

In the summer of 1848, in making some necessary repairs of the pavement in front of the present screen, the underside of what appeared a common slab was found to be richly sculptured with sacred imagery. This led to further investigation, and a very considerable number of fragments of sculpture, in the style of the thirteenth century, and of most surpassing beauty, were discerned. These had formed portions of the ancient jubé, and had been used on its demolition as common materials for flooring the church!

From these remains the design of this magnificent screen can be ascertained with considerable accuracy. The front must have consisted of circular pillars, with richly-foliated caps, supporting arches, surmounted with a succession of subjects carved in alto-relief, and representing the life and passion of our Lord, interspersed with images of prophets, patriarchs, and apostles. The whole was richly painted and gilt.

CATHÉDRALE D'ALBI.

The jubé of this cathedral is fortunately still standing, and nearly in all its original beauty. It is remarkable in its construction, having three doors, beside the two recesses anciently filled with altars, and there is a sort of aisle running round between the main pillars of the choir and the screen of enclosure.

CATHÉDRALE D'AUTUN.

"Before the year 1765, the choir was enclosed by a fine screen of mediæval design, but this was pulled down to make some pretended improvements in the choir, and at the same time a most curious zodiac, illustrating the seasons, &c., executed by a monk named Martin, at the order of Bishop Stephen, which was found in mosaic in the pavement of the choir, was totally destroyed, as well as several other objects of the highest interest." — Chapuy, pp. 9 and 10.

CATHEDRALE DE SENLIS.

The ancient jubé was demolished during the revolution, and the present screen is a miserable erection of *this century*. I have figured it as a specimen of a *modern French screen*, combining every objection that has been raised by the ambonoclasts of our days, without possessing any of the beauties of the ancient works.

CATHEDRAL OF TOULOUSE.

This screen, which I have figured in the plates, was erected in the seventeenth century, and though of debased Italian, is constructed with a rood loft, or jubé, and surmounted by a large crucifix. This jubé is still standing.

CHURCH OF S. SERNIN, TOULOUSE.

The choir of this church is enclosed by iron screens of remarkable design and beautiful execution, figured in the plates.

They are evidently a work of the middle or latter part of the fifteenth century. The lilies and leaves bent up out of the iron plates are produced with wonderful skill. Some of the lateral chapels in the same church have corresponding screen-work, and as Toulouse is a city partaking much of the Spanish character in its buildings, streets, &c., I am inclined to think that it has also borrowed the design of this screen-work from Spain; as Seville, Toledo, and other great churches, have curious iron screens, reaching forty or fifty feet in height, and of a very similar description of work. In the same plate with the Toulouse iron-work, I have figured a screen from the cathedral of Toledo, from which the great similarity of style may be readily perceived.

CATHEDRAL OF AUCH.

The jubé was constructed during the early part of the sixteenth century, in the style of the Renaissance, enriched with most elaborate arabesques and details of the period, and provided with lateral altars. It is still standing, although some attempts have been made by innovators to remove it; but hitherto the canons have resolutely resisted all propositions for ruining the ancient choir.

CATHEDRAL OF RODEZ, LANGUEDOC.

This jubé, which is still standing, was erected in the early part of the sixteenth century. It is divided into three open arches, by clustered pinnacles, with tabernacle-work and imagery. The centre doorway into choir is surmounted by richly flamboyant tracery; on either side are two altars.

CATHEDRAL OF TROYES.

The jubé was supported by eight pillars; on either side of the choir entrance an altar; it was ascended by a staircase on the Gospel side.

The following notice respecting the jubé occurs in the records of the cathedral:—

"En 1382, le chapitre fit marché pour la construction du jubé avec Henri Nardau et Henri de Bruxelles, moyennant cinq sous par jour, ou un mouton d'or par semaine. La première pierre fut posée et bénie par l'Evêque Pierre d'Arcys, le 22 Avril, 1383; il donna la somme de cinq livres pour présent; l'ouvrage ne fut cependant commencé qu'en 1385, et achevé entièrement qu'en 1400. L'image de S. Pierre, qui était au côté de la porte, fut faite par Maître Drouin de Mantes, moyennant cinq livres, et celle de S. Paul, par Maître Gérard, qui eut six livres; quatre chanoines firent les frais de ces statues.

"On lit dans les comptes de l'œuvre de 1383, l'article suivant, qui prouverait qu'un concours avait été ouvert pour le projet du jubé:—

"'Primo pour ung pourtrait fait en parchemin pour ledit jubé, par Henry de Bruisselles, maçon, don commend. de Messigneurs pour monstrer aux bourgois, et aux ouvriers de la ville encontre ung aultre pourtrait, fait par Michelin le maçon, auquel pourtrait, fait par ledit Henry, lesdiz bourgois et ouvriers se sont tenus pour être le meilleur pour ce paie audit Henry don commend. de Messigneurs, xx s.'"

This screen remained perfect till 1793, when it was destroyed by the revolutionists.

It is worthy of remark that the ancient altar, erected by Bishop Odard Henequin, surrounded with curtains, supported by rods attached to brass pillars surmounted by angels, was demolished by the chapter in 1780, to substitute one of modern design; and within twelve years from that time the clergy were dispersed, and the church in the hands of the infidels.

Behind this high altar was a raised loft of carved wood-work, richly painted and gilt, in which the shrines of S. Helene and S. Savinien were placed. The access to this loft was by a circular staircase on the Gospel side, and a corresponding one to descend on the Epistle, to prevent confusion when great numbers of the faithful visited the relics or the feasts.

The great relics of the Sainte Chapelle, at Paris, were reserved in a similar loft behind the high altar, and the circular staircases, of beautiful design, have been recovered, and restored to their original destination.

ACCOUNT OF THE JUBÉS FORMERLY STANDING IN THE CHURCHES OF TROYES.

That of the cathedral already described.

The jubé of the collegiate church of S. Stephen was constructed in 1549, by Dominic Rocour, a Florentine, and Gabriel Fabro, masons of Troyes. It was composed of three arches, or porticos, of the Corinthian order, surmounted by an attic, decorated with bas-relievi and images. Demolished in 1792.

The jubé of the Cordeliers' church was of stone, supported by Doric pillars, and enriched with gilt ornaments. Demolished with the church in 1793.

The jubé of the Jacobins' church was constructed in wood; the front was decorated with bas-relievi and other ornaments, painted and gilt. It was pulled down, by order of the prior, J. B. Pitras, to open the choir.

The jubé of the abbatial church of S. Martin was also of wood, richly painted and gilt. It was pulled down by order of the prior, François Robin, in the year 1760, as he thought it looked too ancient (il le trouvait trop ancien). Thus, of these rood lofts, three were destroyed by the revolutionists, and two by the bad taste of two unworthy priors of the *eighteenth* century.

The jubé of the parochial church of S. Mary Magdalene yet remains perfect; it is of late date and florid design, but exceedingly beautiful in execution.

The subjoined account, as well as the foregoing details, is taken from Monsr. Arnaud's Voyage dans le Département de l'Aube.[15]

VILLEMAUR.

A most interesting jubé, constructed of wood, and erected in the sixteenth century, is still remaining in the parish church of Villemaur. The front of the loft is divided into eleven panels, each containing a mystery of our Lord's passion,

[15] "Enfin, entre tant de jubés détruits, un seul, le plus riche de tous, celui de l'église paroissiale de la Madeleine, est resté debout. Son existence peut être regardée aujourd'hui comme un problème, si l'on considère les différentes causes qui ont amené la destruction des premiers. Aussi ce n'est pas sans avoir éprouvé quelques mutilations, et sans avoir été menacé plus d'une fois d'une ruine complète, que ce monument a traversé trois siècles, et est parvenu jusqu'à nous. Outre la richesse des détails, sa construction est remarquable; il est absolument plat, et terminé en sous-œuvre par trois culs-de-lampe à jour, et sans aucune apparence de voûte. Chacune des deux faces se compose de trois arcs ou archivoltes, ornées de moulures et de festons à jour, dont les courbes sont réunies par des pommes de pin. La retombée des arcs au milieu reste suspendue en l'air, et se termine par des doubles culs-de-lampe, dont les plus saillants portaient jadis des statues, parmi lesquelles on voyait Saint Longin, tenant la lance, et des anges tenant les autres instruments de la passion. Les clochetons, ornés de fleurons et découpés à jour, que l'on voit dans l'intervalle des archivoltes, abritaient ces statues. Entre les clochetons sur chaque arc, est posé un cadre à plusieurs pans, rempli par des petites figures de saints en bas-relief; autour des cadres le champ est occupé par diverses fleurs et feuilles d'ornement. Au-dessus règne la rampe, ou galerie, qui est entièrement découpée à jour. La forme élégante des fleurs-de-lis couronnées, qu'on y remarque, suffirait pour faire connaître l'âge du monument, si nous ne savions d'ailleurs qu'il fut construit vers 1506, à la même époque où l'on jetait les fondements des tours de la cathédrale. Sur la rampe on voyait autrefois quatre statues qui accompagnaient le Christ; il n'en reste que deux, celle de la Vierge et de Saint Jean. Aux angles il y avait des vases à parfums munis d'un couvercle. A chaque extrémité, le jubé est terminé par une construction, en forme de chapelle, appuyée aux gros piliers du chœur. Ces chapelles sont décorées de chaque côté par un pilastre chargé d'arabesques. Au milieu, il existe un enfoncement considérable, de forme carrée, avec des angles rentrant dans la partie supérieure; cet enfoncement était autrefois rempli par un bas-relief, qui en a été arraché et détruit. Au-dessus on voit trois niches sans statues, dont le haut est terminé par des petits dômes et des pyramides évidés à jour avec beaucoup de délicatesse. L'escalier est habilement disposé à droite sous la première arcade du chœur, de manière à ne pas être aperçu de la nef, et à ne pas gêner le service. Il s'élève sur une base octogone, engagée dans le gros pilier, et autour de laquelle la rampe, formée de petites arcades en ogives, se contourne en formant un encorbellement; le dessous de cette saillie est orné de moulures et de gorges profondes remplies par des feuilles d'ornement et des figures d'animaux fantastiques. Sous ce jubé a été enterré Jean Gualde, ou Gaylde, son auteur; on y voyait autrefois son épitaphe, gravée sur un carreau de marbre. Il s'y désignait lui-même par la qualité de maistre maçon, semblait nous donner une garantie de la solidité de son ouvrage, en ajoutant qu'il attendait dessous la resurrection bienheureuse sans crainte d'être écrasé. Le jubé de la Madeleine a de largeur, compris les deux chapelles qui en font partie, trente-six pieds, et de hauteur, jusqu'au haut de la rampe, dix-neuf pieds dix pouces."

carved in bas-relief; below these are a series of arches springing from pendants. The screen is open, with mullions richly carved in the arabesque style, and the loft is ascended by a circular staircase on the Epistle side, enclosed with open mullions. The arrangement of this staircase greatly resembles that of the rood loft at Lambader, in Brittany.

S. GERMAIN DE L'AUXERROIS, PARIS, PARISH CHURCH.

"The jubé is admirable.[16] Clagni was the architect, and Jean Goujon the sculptor. It is composed of three arches supported on Corinthian pillars, the centre one forming the entrance of the choir, and the two side ones chapels with altars. Above the parapet are images of the four Evangelists, and under the cross a fine bas-relief of Nicodemus entombing our Lord." — Sauval, Histoire des Antiquités de la Ville de Paris: tom. i. p. 304. Paris, 1724.

This screen was demolished in the great revolution.

S. ETIENNE DU MONT, PARIS, PARISH CHURCH.

"The jubé erected by Biart is a fine work, the staircases by which it is ascended are most skilful in construction, but it is rather overloaded with ornament." — Ibid. tom. i. p. 407.

This screen, erected at the end of the sixteenth century, is still standing.

BOURGES.

The choir of this church was formerly enclosed by a screen of wood, extending across the nave, on which were thirty brass candlesticks standing in large basins for wax-lights on great feasts.

This screen was provided with three doors, and the front was enriched with sculptures representing the life and passion of our Lord. The whole was demolished in 1774.

NOTRE DAME, PARIS.

Claude Malingre, in his Histoire de Paris, gives the following description of the enclosure of the choir of this church. "The choir is enclosed by a solid wall, but open with pierced work round the high altar, above which are represented sacred personages gilt and painted. The upper screen represents the history of the New Testament, and below, the Old, with scriptures explaining the subjects.

"The great rood which is over the entrance of the choir, is all of one piece,[17] and a chef-d'œuvre of sculpture.

"Below this, on the south side, is an image of the Blessed Virgin held in great

[16] This is Sauval's description.

[17] This must be a mistake of the historian: a crucifix of these dimensions could not possibly be worked in one piece of timber; but it was a very vulgar error to attach great importance to the idea of tabernacle-work, &c. being worked out of a single block or piece; recent investigation has shown the absurdity of these ideas.

devotion, and on the altar is another image of our Lady, called Notre Dame de Consolation, and near it the image of an archbishop with this scripture, 'Noble homme Guillaume de Melun, archevesque de Sens, a fait faire ceste histoire entre ces deux pilliers, en l'honneur de Dieu, de Nostre Dame, et de Monseigneur S. Estienne.'

"On the north side, opposite the Porte Rouge, is an image of a man kneeling, with the following inscription on a label:

"'C'est Maistre Jean Ravy qui fut masson de Notre Dame de Paris, pour l'espace de xxvi. ans, et commença ces nouvelles histoires: et Maistre Jean de Bouteillier les a parfaites en l'an MCCCLI.'"

A great portion of these sculptures still remain, but the choir-screen or jubé described by Malingre must have been demolished in the alterations consequent on the ill-judged vow of Louis XIII., as an old view of the interior of this church, published in the seventeenth century, represents a jubé of a Rococo style, similar to the wood-work of the choir. It was composed of four large piers with four engaged pillars to each: between these, the centre space was filled by two open metal-work gates, and two lateral ones were occupied as usual by altars, but in a most degenerate style of decoration. This screen was so similar to some that I have engraved of a corresponding period, as at Sens, &c., that I have not thought it necessary to do more than give a description of its arrangement. It was demolished in the great revolution of 1790, and has been replaced since the restoration of religion by a very meagre railing and dwarf marble wall.

It is proper to observe that the tradition of the ambones is still retained in two rostrums on either side of the western extremity of the choir, on which the Epistle and Gospel are sung on all great feasts and Sundays.

ABBEY OF FECAMP.

"The length of this church appears at first sight out of all proportion to its width, but this is caused by the destruction of the great screen which separated the choir from the nave. This splendid work, commenced in the year 1500 by Robert Chardon, monk of the abbey, and of exquisite lightness of design, and covered with admirable sculptures, was barbarously demolished by the Vandals of 1802." —Essai sur l'Abbaye de Fécamp, par Leroux de Lincy. Rouen, 1840.

CATHEDRAL CHURCH OF BAYEUX.

"The screen worked in Caen stone was a gift of the late Monsr. de Mesmond. It is supported by six pillars of black marble, given by Canon Baucher; it was commenced in 1698, and completed in 1700. Between the pillars are excellent statues of the Blessed Virgin and S. Joseph, and the whole is surmounted by an image of our Lord crucified, boldly carved. It was erected on the 23rd of December, 1702." — Histoire de la Ville de Bayeux, par M. Beziers. Caen, 1773.

N.B. The original screen was irreparably injured by the Calvinists, who sacked this noble church in 1561. A full account of the sacrilege committed by them, may be seen in the same work, p. 236.

S. RIQUIER, NEAR ABBEVILLE.

The original screen of this magnificent church was demolished, together with the ancient choir fittings, by an unworthy abbot of the eighteenth century; but even at that period, a screen of some kind was considered indispensable, and one of wrought iron, about eighteen feet high, was set up. I have figured this in the plates as a curious specimen of the period.

S. WULFRAN, NEAR ABBEVILLE.

There is a rococo iron screen of about the same date as that at S. Riquier, and probably executed by the same smiths. It is divided into three compartments, with the gates in the centre.

ON SCREENS IN BRITTANY.

S. FIACRE LE FAOUET.

This remarkable rood loft, which I have figured in the plates, is worked in oak, and has been richly painted. The arrangement of the crucifix, and images of our Blessed Lady and St. John, is very singular, as they are placed in front of the loft, instead of being elevated above it. The two thieves are also represented, as is usual in the Crucifixions and Calvaries in Brittany. The crosses to which they are attached are composed of branches of trees.

On the Epistle side the Fall of Man caused by the first Eve, and on the opposite angle the Redemption of Man, through the second Eve, the Blessed Virgin, to whom the angel is announcing the mystery of the incarnation.

There are several very curious carvings in the frieze, among which the popular subject of the mass of S. Martin is easily distinguished.

The church which contains this very curious rood loft is situated in a remote locality, and almost deserted; but a few years since, this venerable relic of ancient piety and art was actually on the point of being sold, had not a neighbouring innkeeper, who derived no small profit from the lovers of antiquity, whom this screen brought to his house, so resolutely opposed its removal, that it was at length suffered to remain.

LAMBADER.

This screen, which is beautifully preserved, with flamboyant tracery, is remarkable for the spiral staircase by which it is ascended, supported by slender shafts, and most ingeniously constructed; the wood groining under the rood loft is bad in principle, as savouring too much of stone construction; but the front of the loft is elaborately carved with tabernacle-work and imagery.

FOLGOET.

This screen, equally remarkable for the elegance of the design as the beauty of its sculptured enrichments, is divided into three compartments, consisting of open cusped arches, supported by pillars, with images, under tabernacle-work, which run up above the arches, and terminate in niches and pinnacle-work. The spaces between this and the canopy-work over arches is filled with quatrefoil-work.

There are two altars on either side of the entrance door, and the space between this and the arch is filled with open tracery-work, like windows.

There are numerous screens yet remaining in many of the churches of Brittany, and originally they were to be found in all. Many others of great interest might be described, but those selected are sufficient to illustrate the argument.

Plate XI.

Iron Screen, Choir of St. Sernin, Toulouse.

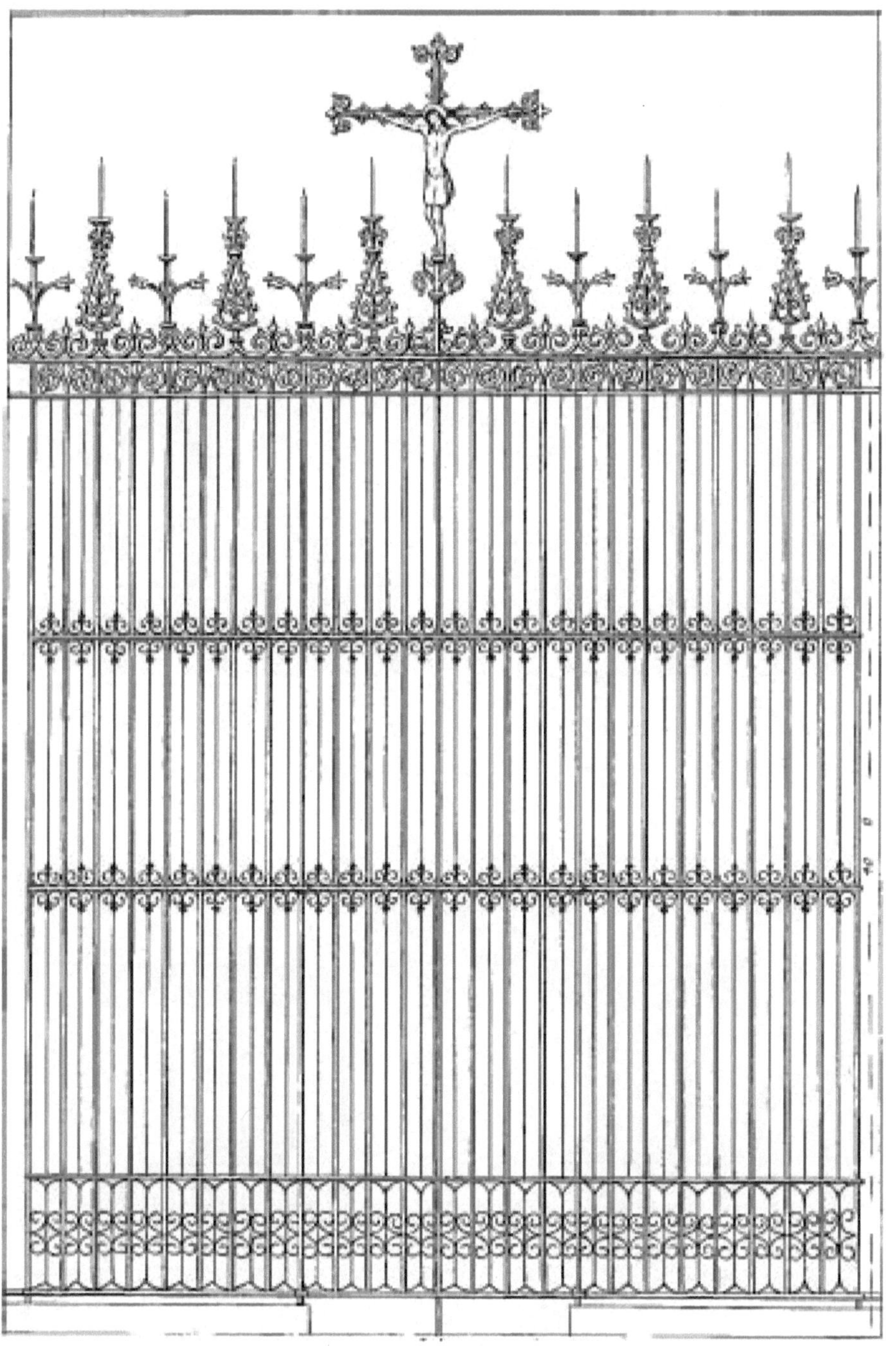

Iron Screen, at Toledo.

St. Paul, Trois Chateaux, Dauphiné.

Screen in S. Agnes, Picardy.

Screens erected in the 18th. Century.

Plate XII.

Soissons.

Screen in the Cathédrale de Sens.

Screens erected in the 18th. Century.

Screen in S. Folgoet.
Screen in Chapelle St. Germain, in Ribermont.
Screens in Brittany.

Screen in S. Fiacre le Faouet.
Plan of Jubé, Notre Dame de l'Epine (Lépine).
Screens in Brittany.

Plate XIV.

Lambader Brittany.

Iron Screen at St. Riquier. 18th Century.

Wooden Screen in the Church of Urnes, near Bergen.

ON SCREENS IN ENGLAND.

There is no country in Christendom where so many screens are still preserved and standing, as in England. Till within a very recent period, every cathedral church had retained its ancient separation between the nave and choir; but sad to relate, one of the most venerable of our churches is now denuded of this most essential and ancient portion of the fittings of a cathedral. I refer to Durham: where choir and nave are thrown into one great vacant space, and all the dignity and reverence of choir worship, suited to a capitular body, destroyed. Although the screen was of most debased design, and erected by a Pagan architect (Inigo Jones), at a Pagan period; yet, being placed in the old and proper position, and having attained a respectable colour, through age, it did its work, and was ten times preferable to the modern vacuum caused by its removal. Indeed, all the alterations at Durham are so many enormities. For centuries the western doors of the cathedral were closed, a chapel built outside them, termed the Galilee, and an altar, dedicated in honour of the Blessed Virgin, stood in the recess of the centre door, but lately, without any reason, for, as I have before said, no entrance can be obtained to the church from that end, have these doors been opened, and the remains of the altar removed, thus destroying one of the most curious traditions belonging to this venerable cathedral. Even the old Cromwellian Puritans did not injure the church so much as *its present restorers*, and it is greatly to be regretted that there are no means to compel these authorities to desist from their insane innovations. In the eyes of all true ecclesiologists Durham has lost half its apparent length, half its grandeur, since it has lost its screen, and it has got somewhat of the conventicle. But to return—York, Lincoln, Southwell, Wells, Exeter, Bristol, Chichester, Canterbury, Rochester, Chester, Norwich,[18] have all their old screens and rood-lofts standing. These are too well known amongst persons interested in this subject to need detailed description, but I may observe that they nearly all are ascended by staircases in the thickness of the eastern walls, rising up on each side, and that lateral altars in the screens were not so common as on the continent. The roods, in all cases, have been replaced by organs, which are badly placed both as regards the chanters and the effect of the building. The only instance I have ever met with the remains of a rood is at Columpton, near Exeter, where a large block of oak, carved like rock-work, with a skull and bones, evidently intended to represent Calvary, is still left, and in its upper part a deep mortice to receive the end of the rood.

Our parochial churches are yet rich in screens; of wooden rood-lofts we may particularize Sleaford, Newark, Bury St. Edmunds, Fairford, Tong, Lanryst, Sefton,

---

[18] Till very recently there were distinct traces of the side altars under this screen, but they have been removed, and modern tracery put in their place.

Ranworth, and Southwold as some amongst the most remarkable. The countries most abounding in screens, are Norfolk, Suffolk, Lincolnshire, Cambridgeshire, and Devonshire, but each county presents many interesting examples, and it must be distinctly understood that every church, small or great, was originally provided with a screen.

In Norfolk, the churches of Cawston, Sall, N. Walsham, Worsted, Walcot, Trunch, Happisburgh, Bacton, Paston, Lynn, Ranworth, Cley, Castle Acre, Cressingham, Snetisham, and Ackle, &c., have all fine screens. Many of them are richly painted, and the lower panels filled with images of saints on gold and diapered grounds. The best preserved are those at Ranworth and Cawston. About five different painters were employed in the decoration of these, as the various styles may be distinctly traced over various parts of the country. Some of them exhibit far greater skill than others, but all have a deal of quaint character, and the images fill up the spaces in which they are placed, by the adjustment of drapery, &c.

There is a great deal of fine screen-work in Suffolk, at Woolpitt, Elmswell, Thurston, Lavenham, Long Melford, Brandon, Southwold, Blythburgh, Hawsted, and many other churches.

In Lincolnshire there are splendid screens at Winthorpe, Ingoldmills, Orby, Burgh, Croft, Boston, Hackington, Swineshead, Tattershall, Ewerby, Newark, Grantham.

In Devonshire the screens have been generally preserved, and on many of them the painted panels with saints and imagery are quite perfect. They are mostly constructed on one principle, with projecting wooden ribbed-work crossing the rood-loft; at Honiton, Feniton, Bradwinch, West Buckland, Columpton, Dartmouth, Kenton, Pinhoe, Plymtree, Tollaton, Tiverton, Atherington, Dawlish, &c., are screens surmounted by rood-lofts; but at Bridford, Burlescombe, Clayhanger, Dartington, Hempston, Plymstock, West Ogwell, &c., there are only screens without lofts, but of exceedingly elaborate design, and for the most part richly painted and gilt, some with saints in the lower panels, like those in Norfolk. A very numerous list, indeed, might be made of churches in this country, where screens of some kind are to be found; they are not always of the same material, for the examples of stone are numerous, as at Totness, Culmstock, Colyton, and Paignton, &c., this latter being monumental, and containing family tombs, introduced in the screen-work. Although the counties above mentioned are those which abound the most in fine examples of screen-work, yet most numerous and interesting specimens may be found in every county.

Sefton church, in Lancashire, has a splendid rood and side screens enclosing the chancel, of a later period, but most elaborate detail.

The parish church at Lancaster contains some very magnificent screen and canopy-work of the time of Edward I. The treatment of the crockets is quite peculiar, as they are joined together, forming a sort of solid enrichment on the gablets.

The priory church of Hexham is rich in carved fittings. The stalls and screen-work of the choir are perfect, and though rude in execution are extremely interesting; this being a conventual church, the screen-work is quite solid. If we proceed further north, we shall find the same system of enclosure of choirs and chancels by screens. The rood-loft at Glasgow is still perfect, and though the Scotch churches have been horribly mutilated, the ancient position of the enclosures is to be traced in most of them.

The churches in Wales were mostly furnished with rood-lofts. The screen and loft at Lanryst are most elaborate in carved enrichments; they were probably erected in the beginning of the fifteenth century, and it is worthy of remark that in this, as well as others, there is a striking similarity between the screens in Wales and Brittany.

Were it not tedious, I could supply a long list of fine screens yet remaining in every part of the country, but there are few of an older date than the thirteenth century, as so many of these churches have been rebuilt or refitted since that period. There can be no doubt that even the Saxon churches were provided with some enclosure across the arch which divided off the chancel. Indeed, so natural and right does it seem to have this separation, that the principles of screens survived the Reformation, as will be mentioned hereafter. But not only do we find the cathedrals and parochial churches to have been furnished with screens, but also chapels in private houses and hospitals for the poor. The archbishop's chapel at Croydon is divided by a plain but very substantial and effective screen, figured in the first volume of Pugin's examples.

Browne's hospital at Stamford, Bishop Bubwith's almshouses at Wells, S. John's hospital at Sherburne, the bede-houses at Northampton and Leicester, the Vicar's chapel at Wells, have all screens in their chapels, and some of them of most elegant design. In the private chapel of an ancient mansion at Cothele, on the banks of the Tamar, is an open screen of perpendicular work. In short, I do not imagine that any building dedicated to divine worship was considered complete, unless furnished with a suitable screen.

In the reign of Edward VI., the roods, with their attendant images, were removed, and it is probable that the lofts were stript at the same time of the candlesticks and basons of latten, wherein the lights were set up. But the screens themselves do not appear to have suffered, and indeed, in accordance with the decree that the chancels were to remain as in time past, the screens were absolutely necessary. Considering the great number of screens yet standing, it is evident that those which have been removed, were demolished, through the ignorance or indifference of the authorities during the repairs that the buildings have undergone, and I am personally acquainted with several instances which corroborate this fact. There are several examples of post-Reformation screens, one at Gedington church, of a simple but good character, and another at Martham church, Norfolk, which is painted and gilt.

The choir of Wimborne Minster, Dorsetshire, was fitted up in the beginning of the seventeenth, or end of the sixteenth century, quite after the old traditions, as regards screen-work and arrangement, though the details were of course debased.

The collegiate chapels of the universities present several remarkable examples of post-Reformation screens, as Wadham, Baliol, Lincoln, the old screen of Magdalene, before the recent alterations, at Oxford; and Peterhouse, Caius college, Clare-hall, at Cambridge; even the screen of King's college chapel itself was not erected till after the schism, as the initials of Anna Boleyn occur in its decorations.

I have been informed of a screen in one of the churches at Leeds, erected in the seventeenth century; and an oak screen of a still later date is standing in the church of St. Peter, upon Cornhill, London. Lady Dudley, a most pious lady, in the time of Charles I. set up a screen in the church of St. Giles-in-the-fields, which was af-terwards destroyed by the Puritan faction. The whole transaction is so illustrative of the spirit of those times, and so applicable to the fanatics of our own days, that I have printed it at length at p. 74.

From these instances it will be seen that the principle of screening off chan-cels has been retained in the church of England since its separation from Catholic unity, and the partial discontinuance in the eighteenth century was purely owing to extreme ignorance of ecclesiastical traditions, which prevailed throughout the members of this communion at that period, remarkable only for debased taste, and a total disregard of the wonderful productions of Catholic antiquity.

To this brief account of screens in England, I have subjoined some interesting extracts from churchwardens' accounts and other documents, printed in Nichol's illustrations, which will illustrate their history and decoration.

ACCOUNTS OF ST. MARGARET'S, WESTMINSTER.

"1510.

> "Item. The said wardens, now accomptants, received of Mrs. Elizabeth Morley, widow, towards the new making of a Rood, Mary, and John, in the roodeloft, at the time the parish be of pow-er and substance, to build and make the same rood loft, the sum of £10. 0s. 0d.

> "Item. Received of the gift of Watir Gardynar, to the making of the rode-loft in the middle isle within the church, as more plainly appeareth by acquittance made by the said churchwardens to the said N. Watir, dated the ... day of October, the 9e yere of the reign of King Henry VII., £38. 0s. 0d."

The next item occurs in the reign of Edward VI.—

> "Paid to Thomas Stockdale, of XXXV ells of cloth for the frunte of the rood-lofte, whereon the commandments be written...."

It appears from this, that the commandments were set up originally in the rood lofts, and not over the altars. But in the succeeding reign of Mary, this cloth, on which the commandments were painted, was turned to a different purpose, for in 1557, we find the following item:

> "For making iii serplys of the cloth that hung before the rode loft, written with the commandments, 2s. 0d."

In 1559, the rood was destroyed, and in a barbarous manner, for we find the following items:

"Paid to John Rial for his iii days' work to take down the roode, Mary, and John, 2s. 8d.

"Item. To the same for cleaving and sawing of the rood, Mary, and John, 1s."

In 1561, "Paid to joyners and labourers about the taking down and new re-forming of the rood loft, as by a particular book thereof made doth appear, £37. 10s. 2d."

This is the last item which occurs respecting the rood loft of this church.

S. LAWRENCE, READING.

From Coate's History of Reading.

"1499.

"It. Rec. at Alhalow-tyde for the rode light xs. iiiid.

"It. Payed for xliii.-li. of ire wark, on the south end of the rode loft to stay the lyght, the li. iid. Sma. viis. iid.

"It. Payed for xxvi. li. of irewark on the north syde or end of the same rode loft to stay the same lyght, pic le li., ii. Sma. iiiis. iiiid.

"It. Payed for lyne to draw the curtens in the same lofte, iiid.

"It. Payed for scouring of the laten bolls in the said loft, iiiid.

"It. Payed for six laten bolls on the north side of the rode loft, viiis.

"1506.

"It. Paied for settyng up of the said rode, Mary, and John, for the remouing of the organs, and for making ye sete for ye player of ye same organs, xxd.

"It. Paied to Henry Blanksten, paynt for gilding the rode, Mary, and John, in the rode loft, xiiiis."

EXTRACTS FROM THE CHURCHWARDEN'S ACCOMPTS OF ST. MARY HILL, LONDON.

Costs paid for penting of the roodes, with karvying, and oder costs also.

"1497.

"Item. To Sir John Plomer, for makying of the fyugyrrs of the roode, £0. 1s. 8d.

"Item. To the karvers for makyg of iii. dyadems,[19] and of oon of the Evangelists, and for mendyg the roode, the crosse, the Mary

---

[19] *Diadem*, the old English word for Nimbus.

and John, the crown of thorn, with all odir fawts, £0. 10s. 0d.

"Item. To Undirwood, for peynting and gyldyng of the roode, the crosse, Mary and John, iiii. Evangelists, and the iii. dyadems, with the nobills that I owe to him in money, £5.

"Item. For makyng clene of standards, candlesticks, braunches, with the bolls of laten upon the beame of the rodeloft, anenst the fest of Est., A.D., 1486."

EXTRACTS FROM THE CHURCHWARDENS' ACCOMPTS OF THE PARISH OF ST. HELEN'S, ABINGDON.

"1555.

"Payde for making the roode and peynting the same, £0. 5s. 4d..

"For making the roode lyghtes, £0. 10s. 6d..

"For the roode lyghtes at Christmase, £1. 3s. 2½d..

"1557.

"Received of the paryshe for the roode lyghts at Christmas. Payde for peynting the roode of Marie and John, and the patron of the churche, £0. 6s. 8d..

"For the roode, Marie, and John, with the patron of the church, £0. 18s. 0d.

"1561.

"To the somner, for bringing the order for the roode loft.

"To the carpenter and others for taking down the roode lofte, and stopping the holes in the wall, where the joices stoode, £0. 15s. 8d.

"To the peynter, for writing the scripture where the roode loft stoode, and overthwarte the same isle, £0. 3s. 4d."

EXTRACTS FROM THE CHURCHWARDENS' ACCOMPTS OF HEYBRIDGE.

"Payde for waxe for the roode-lofte light agenst Chrystemas last paste, pryce the pounde 10d., £0. 4s. 2d.

"A cloth of the Passyon to hang in the roode lofte in Lente."

EXTRACTS FROM THE CHURCHWARDENS' ACCOMPTS OF WALBERSWICK.

"Item. Paide to Robt. Bungyng, for helpyng of oon borde in the roode lofte, £0. 0s. 2d.

"Item. Payd for mendyng and staying ye roodeloft, in hale, £0. 0s. 2d.

"Item. To ye said Stephin, for mendyng ye herne wark in ye rode lofte, £0. 0s. 4d."

EXTRACTS FROM THE CHURCHWARDENS' ACCOMPTS OF WOODBRIDGE.

"Hic jacet Johannes Albred quondam Twelewever, istius ville. Ob. primo die Maii, 1400, et Agnes uxor eijus.

"This Twelewever, with Agnes, his wife, were at the charges (people of all degree being, as then, forward to beautifie the house of God), to cut, gild, and paint a rood loft or partition betwixt the body of the church and the quire, whereon the pictures of the crosse and crucifixe, the Virgin Mary, of angels, archangels, saints and martyrs are figured to the life: which how glorious it was when it was all standing, may be discerned by that which remaineth. This, their work of pietie, was depensild [painted] upon the fabricke, of which so much as is left.

"'Orate.—Johannes Albrede et Agnetis—Soluerunt pro pictura totius hujus operis superne:—videlicet, crucis crucifixi, Marie, archangelorum et totius candeleb.'

"The names of some of the saints pourtraied upon the worke and yet remaining, are these, S. Paul, S. Edward, S. Kenelm, S. Oswald, S. Cuthbert, S. Blaze, S. Quintin, S. Leodegare, S. Barnaby, S. Jerome."—From Weever's Funeral Monuments.

ACCOUNT OF THE SCREEN IN THE CHURCH OF ST. GILES-IN-THE-FIELDS.

"The said church is divided into three parts: the sanctum sanctorum being one of them, is separated by a large skreene in the figure of a beautiful gate in which is carved two large pillars and three large statues: on the one side is Paul with his sword; on the other Barnabas with his book; and over these, Peter with his keys; they are all set above with winged cherubims, and beneath supported by lions.

"This screen, which was erected by the pious munificence of Lady Dudley, about ten years previous, was demolished by the Puritans in 1644. We find a party in the parish in 1640, exhibiting articles to Parliament against the rector, Dr. Heywood. It was stated that, in the parish church were set up crucifixes, and divers images of saints, and likewise organs with other confused musicke, hindering devotion." The screen given by Lady Dudley was also decreed as superstitious, and in 1644 is the following memorandum respecting it: "Also, we, the auditors of this account, doe find that the accomptant, Edward Gerrard, was commanded, by ordinance of Parliament, to take down the screene in the chancell, it being found superstitious, which was accordingly done, and it sold for fortye shillings;

"Also, out of the receipt for church goods, were paid the bricklayer for mending the walls on both sides the chancel, where the screen stood."—From Parton's

History of St. Giles-in-the-Fields.

It is remarkable what a similarity of feeling against screens is to be found among Puritans and Paganisers.

OF THE FOUR CLASSES
OF AMBONOCLASTS.

THE CALVINIST AMBONOCLAST.

When we now behold the city of London, with its narrow lanes, lined with lofty warehouses and gloomy stores, leading down to the banks of the muddy Thames, whose waters are blackened with foul discharges from gas-works and soap-boilers, while the air is darkened with the dense smoke of chimneys rising high above the parish steeples, which mark the site of some ancient church, destroyed in the great conflagration, it is difficult to realize the existence of those venerable and beautiful fabrics where the citizens of London assembled in daily worship, and whose rood lofts shone so gloriously on Easter and Christmas feasts. But this great and ancient city was inferior to none in noble religious buildings; and in the sixteenth century the traveller who approached London from the west, by the way called Oldbourne, and arriving at the brow of the steep hill, must have had a most splendid prospect before him; to the right the parish church of S. Andrew's, rising most picturesquely from the steep declivity, and surrounded by elms, with its massive tower, decorated nave, and still later chancel; on the left the extensive buildings of Ely-house, its great gateway, embattled walls, lofty chapel and refectory, and numerous other lodgings and offices, surrounded by pleasant gardens, as then unalienated from the ancient see after which it was called, it presented a most venerable and ecclesiastical appearance. Further in the same direction might be perceived the gilded spire of S. John's church of Jerusalem and the Norman towers of S. Bartholomew's priory. Immediately below was the Fleet river, with its bridge, and the masts of the various craft moored along the quays. At the summit of the opposite hill, the lofty tower of S. Sepulchre's, which though greatly deteriorated in beauty, still remains. In the same line, and over the embattled parapets of the Newgate, the noble church of the Grey Friars, inferior in extent only to the cathedral of S. Paul, whose gigantic spire, the highest in the world, rose majestically from the centre of a cruciform church nearly seven hundred feet in length, and whose grand line of high roofs and pinnacled buttresses stood high above the group of gable-houses, and even the towers of the neighbouring churches. If we terminate the panorama with the arched lantern of S. Mary-le-Bow, the old tower of S. Michael, Cornhill, and a great number of lesser steeples, we shall have a faint idea of the ecclesiastical beauty of Catholic London. But to return to our more immediate subject, each of these fine churches was provided with its screen and rood. Numerous are the entries in the old churchwardens' accounts yet remaining of pious offerings made by the citizens to beautify the devotional sculptures which decorated them, and to provide tapers and branches to deck them for the return-ing festivals. There were veils for Lent, when the glory of our Lord was partially obscured by his approaching Passion; and there were garlands for Easter, and pas-chal lights, and crowns, and diadems. The old parish church of S. Mary-at-Hill was inferior to none in the beautiful partition of its chancel; it was principally the work of a pious citizen, who, on the decay of the older work, renewed the same; or, as the old chronicle expresses it:—"For the love he bore to Jesu and his holy Modir did sett up at his own proper costes and charges, and most artificially dispensil, the image of Christ, Mary, and John, and many saynts and aungels, with the loft whereon they stood: and for the due maintainyng of a perpetual light to hang brenyng before the same, and for a priest to synge at his anniversary he also left two tenements in the paryshe of Barkynge; and when he died he was buried under a grey stone, over and against the holy doors of the chancel, and till the sad time of the civil wars, was his portraieture in brass, and that of his wife, and 3 sons and 5 daughters at their feet, and his shield of mark, and the arms of the honourable Company of the Fishmongers, and round the bordure, with an Evangelist at every corner, was this inscription: '✠ Good Christen people, of your charitie pray for the soulys of John Layton, citizen and fyshemonger of London, who deceeded on the feast of S. Stephen, in the yeare of our Lorde 1456, and of Margaret his wyffe, on whose sowlys and the sowlys of Christen men may Jesu have mercy. Pater, ave, Amen.'" And on the brestsumer of the rood loft were carved divers devices, such as S. Peter's keys for his Patron, and dolphins and sea-luces salterwise for the Company, and scrolls, with **Lays** coming out of tuns for the founder, and above all was a most artificial bratishing, with large bowls of brass, with prickets for tapers on great feasts, and there was a staircase of freestone, closed by an oak door, set up on the south side of the aisle, for the convenience of ascending to the same; and on each of the lower panels of the holy doors and of the bays of the screen were pictures of saints and martyrs, on grounds of gold diaper, each with their legend. For nearly a century this goodly work had stood the pride and delight of the parishioners, who bestowed much cost on sustaining its lights and ornaments, as the church books yet testify. But a sad and fearful change was approaching—new and heretical doctrines were circulated and even heard at Paul's Cross; men became divided in heart and mind; the returning festivals exhibited no unity of joy and devotion; many gloomily stayed away; and it was currently reported that nocturnal meetings were privately held at some citizens' houses, where preachers from beyond sea taught novel opinions, and inveighed against altars and priests, and sacred images and ancient rites; and soon there was a quest to examine into the ornaments of the churches, and many a goodly pyx, and chalice, and chris-matory were seized by the sacrilegious spoilers for the state; and shortly after the ancient service was interrupted by scoffers and infidels, and they who adhered to the old faith of England's church were filled with sorrow and dismay, and they worshipped in fear and sadness, and every day brought new troubles and greater sacrilege.

It was late in the evening, or rather the early part of the night, that a number of persons, evidently of very varied ranks and conditions, were crowded into a back chamber in the habitation of a citizen notoriously disaffected to the ancient religion; they were listening with considerable earnestness of attention, to the exhortations, or rather ravings, of a man of sour aspect, whose dress and gestures announced him as belonging to the class of unordained preachers called the New Gospellers. The subject of his discourse was the extirpation of idolatry; the triumphs of the Jewish people over the unbelieving nations was the principal source from whence he drew his denunciations. The texts relating to the destruction of the heathen idols he transferred to the ancient images of the church, and succeeded in rousing the passions of his hearers to the utmost frenzy. "But why," he exclaimed, "do we waste time? Let us lay the axe to the root of the tree; the famous rood of S. Mary-at-Hill standeth hard by, to the shame and reproach of Christian men. Let us pluck it down and utterly deface it, so it perish and be seen no more." Some of the most zealous of the fanatics instantly acted on this suggestion. Descending to the street, they soon surrounded the residence of the aged sacrist (who still retained his office, though the duties were sadly curtailed), and rousing him from his rest, demanded the keys of the church. Alarmed by the uproar, many casements were opened; but the numbers of the clamouring party appeared so considerable, and the prospect of any assistance from the watch (which was then only perambulatory) so remote, that none ventured down to the assistance of the old clerk, who, terrified by the menaces of his assailants, and without any companion except a lad who acted as his servant, at length surrendered the keys. A few links had by this time been procured, and by their smoky and lurid light the southern door was opened, and the whole party tumultuously crowded into the venerable edifice. The lamp so liberally provided by John Layton had ceased to burn for some time; its revenue had been sequestered as superstitious, and the chancel was shrouded in impenetrable darkness. Against this gloomy background the rood and its attendant images stood out in red reflected light, but the Jews themselves that scoffed on Calvary's mount were not more bitter in their scorn than the New Gospellers, who uttered loud shouts and cries as they beheld the object of their sacrilegious vengeance. The sound of hollow blows echoes through the church, the lower door is forced: ascending footsteps are heard on the staircase; then the rebounding tread of heavy feet on the loft itself, torches appear—axes gleam— heavy blows fall thick; some cleave, some pierce, some shout, and with one great crash it totters and falls—images, cross—all lie a ruin on the ancient pavement. The work of destruction now proceeds: some wrench the extended limbs from the sculptured cross; broken and dismembered, the sacred image of the Redeemer is dragged down the nave; while others deface and cleave the evangelistic symbols, tossing the fragments in wild derision; some curse, some spit, some foam, others exclaim, "Into the fire with it!" and a glare of light striking through the western window, showed that the suggestion had been followed; it crackled in the garth, and now the mangled images are piled on the roaring mass, while furious cries, "Away with it! Destroy it utterly!" break through the stillness of the night, and scare the affrighted parishioners, who behold this horrible spectacle from their gabled residences. Nearly three hundred years have elapsed, and the rood was again raised in glory in this very city, and the cry "Away with it!" was again heard. Came it from the blaspheming Jews? No. Came it from the bitter Calvinists? No. Came it from the incarnate fiends? No. It proceeded from a *modern Catholic ambonoclast*!!!!

THE PAGAN AMBONOCLAST.

Louis de Chantal was born in France, of noble parents, about the middle of the eighteenth century; being a younger brother, he was destined from his earliest years to the ecclesiastical state, but on arriving at a maturer age, his tastes and inclinations were so adverse to the sacred functions, that he proceeded no further than receiving the tonsure, which enabled him to hold the rich ecclesiastical preferment in the gift of his family, and entitled him to the appellation of Monsieur l'Abbé de Chantal. He soon became commendatory abbot of two once great religious establishments, then languishing under a sad decay of zeal and discipline consequent on the loss of a regular head. The great object of commendatory abbots was to keep the number of religious to the lowest possible amount, in order to profit the more by the revenues, which they diverted to their own private benefit and luxury. At Conques the decay of the temporal kept pace with that of the spiritual; the buildings which, for the most part, had been erected during the glorious period of S. Louis, were falling fast to ruin. The regular portions, now much too large for the habitations of the few religious that remained, exhibited the desolate appearance of neglect and emptiness. Verdure luxuriated in the untrodden courts, and sprung up even in the very cloister, whose vaults had long ceased to echo the regulated tread and solemn chaunt of the ancient Benedictines. It was evident that essential repairs could not long be postponed, and a bull issued by the Pope a few years previous, requiring the conventual buildings of France to be substantially repaired out of the revenues, was still in force. The matter was, however, deferred for a short time, as our young abbé was about to proceed on his travels to the more classic ground of Italy, at that period ignorantly regarded as the great repository and source of all art and taste. The noble mediæval cathedrals of France were considered by Monsieur de Chantal as so many specimens of ancient barbarism, but the extravagancies of Bernini and the distortions of Le Pautre were splendid achievements in his eyes. It may be readily conceived what class of objects arrested his attention in his travels: his enthusiasm on arriving at the Eternal City was boundless—he almost believed that the heathen mythology was revived, and that he was in the presence of those divinities whose exploits had been the study of his early youth. The splendid galleries of voluptuous art, where the metamorphoses and amatory combats of Ovid were depicted to the life. The marble goddesses in shady groves, and sporting tritons cooling the air in high and sparkling jets—the obelisks, the sarcophagi, the endless treasures of classic art. Then even the churches, they were scarcely to be distinguished from the exquisite taste of the heathens themselves. Thinly draperied saints were borne into paradise by hovering Cupids. Voluptuous female statues reclined on the sarcophagi of bishops and ecclesiastics,—herculean martyrs writhed like dying gladiators, while naked angels held aloft the victor's crown. Our abbé was ravished with astonishment and delight as the eager cicerone drew him from one far-famed object to another, each more wonderful than the last. In his perambulations he occasionally passed some venerable looking sanctuaries, but the usual exclamation of the guide, *eh, una porcheria,* was quite sufficient to repress any desire of examining them; and in a word, he returned from Italy like most of the ecclesiastics of that period, with a thorough contempt for the ancient traditions of church architecture, and a determination to

Italianize, as far as possible, in any work with which he might be connected. The time had now arrived when the repairs of the abbey of Conques could be no longer delayed, and accompanied by an architect of the Souflot style, with a thickly curled wig reaching half-way down his shoulders, he one morning started from his hotel at Paris, and proceeded thither. Although only a few leagues distant, the bad roads so delayed their progress, that it was late in the afternoon when they attained the top of the descent that led down into the valley where the abbey was situated. A little to the eastward of the scattered houses which formed the village, and small but characteristic church, stood the then lofty and irregular abbatial buildings. High above the rest rose the long grey mass of the church, surmounted by a high leaden roof, whitened with age. A forest of pinnacles surrounded the apse, while buttress and arc buttant continued in regular succession to surround the vast fabric. At the western end were two towers, but the southern one alone had been carried up to its intended height, the other had received a temporary roof, when raised a few feet above the nave; the abbacy shortly after fell into *commendam*, and it rose no higher. A small but elegant leaded spire was placed at the intersection of the nave and transept, but it was evidently a substitute for some far grander design in the way of a centre lantern, as might be divined by the rising of angle masonry left incomplete.

A dense mass of wood covered the opposite hill with a deep green, while the warm tints of a westerning sun relieved each turret and pinnacle in a glowing hue on the verdant background. A rapid descent soon brought the abbé and his companion to the gates, which were opened with some difficulty to admit the equipage within the first court; such vehicles were utterly unknown when these buildings were raised, and further progress was impossible except on foot. The abbé then alighted, and was received with much external respect by the few religious who remained the occupants of a monastery, where more than a hundred sons of S. Benedict had kept the rule together in older and better times.

The next morning the architect waited on Monsieur de Chantal in his chamber, "Monseigneur," he exclaimed, "j'ai parcouru les bâtimens;—rien de plus gothique, de plus mauvais; point de règles, point de principes; ces gens-là ils n'ont jamais connu le beau; il faut tout démonter, tout démolir." This proposition, however well it might accord with the tastes of the commendatory abbot, was by no means agreeable to his intentions, as the proposed demolition and rebuilding would cost a considerable sum, which he thought might be as well expended on some new gardens attached to his hotel at Paris, and he therefore, on a personal inspection, considerably modified the sweeping intentions of his architect, and confined his operations to indispensable repairs and the erection of some new offices. These points arranged, he proceeded at once to the inspection of the church. On entering by the western cloister door, the venerable fabric appeared nearly in its original state: the nave was divided into nine bays with light clustered shafts, the centre one of each running quite up to receive the groin; the triforium was divided into compartments corresponding to the mullions of the clerestory windows, and filled with imagery and devices in painted glass. The upper windows contained the image of a saint in every light, under a high canopy of rich design. The lower windows of the aisles had been altered in the fifteenth century, the tracery was more elaborately ramified and the glass exhibited a higher degree of pictorial skill, though inferior in severity and style to the more ancient glazing.

The ribs of the groining were richly painted at the intersections, with images in relief on every boss. The pavement was irregularly studded with incised slabs of benefactors, who were permitted to repose beneath the floor of that edifice to whose support and glory they had contributed while living. But the most striking object that presented itself to the sight, was a most elaborate jubé or rood loft, extending completely across the entrance to the choir. Eight slender shafts sustained seven arches, richly crocketted on the labels, with images of angels in sexfoils, filling up the spandrils. Between every arch and over the shafts, was an image standing on a corbel under a projecting tabernacle; immediately over them were sixteen arched and canopied recesses, each containing, in high relief, a mystery of our Lord's life and passion, most artificially wrought in stone, and heightened with gilding and colours, and over all, in the midst, was a great rood rising almost to the vault of the church, with most cunning work of leaves and foliage running up and about it, and sprouting forth at its extremities, and on it an image of our Lord as it were a king with a diadem on his head, and a long tunic, all gilt, reaching down to his feet, with the borders set with crystals, and on either side an image of our Blessed Lady and S. John, and two cherubims with images of gold. This rood, which was held in singular veneration by neighbouring inhabitants, and by them commonly termed Le Bon Dieu de Conques, found but little favour in the eyes of our refined abbé; "Il faut démonter cette vieillerie-là," said he, turning to the architect. "Ah, mon Dieu, oui," was the ready answer, "*ça fera du bien*; on peut y mettre une grillage en fer, comme à S. Denis."[20] —"C'est une bonne idée!" cried Monsieur de Chantal, "et je la ferai exécuter." It is probable that, in carrying out this barbarous and sacrilegious intention, the abbé meant to *improve* the church!! Brought up in the principles of error and paganism, to him nothing was beautiful that did not savour of classic art. It is probable that he really meant well, as far as so debased a mind could mean well; let us hope his ignorance obtained his final pardon, and that he was permitted to expiate in his doleful end this terrible deed of destruction. The religious of Conques mourned most bitterly over the demolition of the ancient jubé. Men who live a religious life are naturally adverse to change: the removal of an image, a picture, an object on which they have been accustomed to look with devotion, is to them an irreparable loss, and great were the wailings of the little community when they learned their abbé's decision; remonstrance was, however, useless against such superior power, and the demolition of the whole was finally decided. But its destruction was not deplored by the religious only,—the inhabitants of Conques, a simple-minded but devout race, had, for many generations, regarded this ancient and edifying imagery with singular veneration. From their early years, succeeding fathers had taught their little ones that the great king upon the cross was the son of the king of kings, who expired on the rood to save them, and there was his blessed mother weeping at his side, and the beloved disciple to whose care she was committed; and below all were wonderful mysteries shown, from the salutation of the angel to the painful

[20] The choir of S. Denis, near Paris, had been modernised a few years previous.

bearing of the cross to Calvary. All these and much more were set forth and most artificially, and great was the lamentation of the good people of Conques when they heard that it was to be no more seen.

Impatient to begin his improvements, the abbé procured some workmen to commence the demolition before his return to Paris. Among those who presented themselves was a young man of great athletic powers, but of a sinister and scornful countenance, and who appeared to proceed in the task of destruction with singular alacrity and energy. Several men with ropes and ladders had now ascended the upper part of the rood, while the young man before mentioned stood at the foot, and alternately applied a crow and axe to cut away the mortice in which the base rested and prise it out. Before the men above had the ropes properly fast to lower all, by a tremendous effort he forced the foot from its socket, and the cross, inclining to the Gospel side, fell over, carrying away the image of the Blessed Virgin in descent, and the whole mass lay broken on the pavement. The movement was so sudden that it startled the abbé, who was standing near the man, and a feeling of dread seemed to appal the other workmen as they gazed on the fallen rood, but the face of the youth was flushed with ill-concealed exultation, which the abbé remarked, and attributed at the time to his successful display of strength; but it came from a far deeper feeling, as he afterwards discerned to his own destruction.

The whole screen was afterwards demolished; and by the end of the succeeding year, when Monsieur de Chantal came to inspect the alterations, he found, to his great satisfaction, that something of the character of a Berninian church had been imparted to the ancient choir. A rococo screen of open iron work, with his own arms in the centre, had supplanted the ancient screen. Pointed arches had been turned into round ones by help of plaster; the ancient capitals, luxuriant in salient foliage and quaint imagery, had been transferred into heavy Corinthians; most of the painted glass had been removed and replaced by large square white panes. The shafts of the pillars were marbled by streaks of paint, and this once perfect choir reduced down to a base and bad imitation of the corrupt Italian style.

About a furlong from the abbey-gate was the old parish church, a simple and unpretending structure, with its slate-topped steeple and gilded cock, a most fitting emblem of the exemplary and vigilant pastor, the Père Duchesne, a venerable priest, who for many years had most faithfully discharged the sacred duties of his cure; a man of most retired habits, who devoted that portion of his time that was not occupied by parochial cares to learned researches and pursuits. He was deeply read in liturgical lore, and held the ancient traditions and offices of the church in great veneration. Every Sunday and feast the most respected of his parishioners assembled round the lectern in the chancel, where they sang the praises of God in the old plain song, for no other music was tolerable to the ears of either priest or people. The interior of the church, though simple, was not devoid of interest. There were considerable remains of painted glass, especially towards the eastern end; the high altar was coeval with the erection of the church itself, and had been traditionally consecrated by a holy bishop, now numbered among the saints of God. The altar of the Lady chapel dated from the end of the fourteenth century, and was erected by a seigneur who lived in the old chateau on the hill, then in ruins. The rood loft was remarkable; the front was supported by four pillars, sustaining three equal arches; the space between these pillars was enclosed by a sort of iron trellis, set up with the original work, as a protection to two side altars, the reredoses of which formed a solid wall for nearly six feet high, and were then divided by mullions into lights, like a window; these were also secured by bars, and a massive pair of doors, with rich ornamental iron-work, closed the entrance to the chancel. I have been thus particular in the description of this screen, as it is important for a subsequent part of this history. Such was the church, and such its curé. The Abbé de Chantal, in ordinary courtesy to the old priest, determined to call at his residence previous to his departure. On arriving, he was ushered into a small chamber, where the curé was seated with a folio extended on the table before him. Somewhat surprised at the sudden entrance of the abbé, and not over well pleased, as he held such quasi ecclesiastics at the lowest estimation, he begged to know the reason for so unlooked-for a visit. "Oh, Monsieur le curé," carelessly exclaimed the abbé, "I have been making great improvements at the abbey, and I wish to know if you have seen what has been done?" "I have, indeed, seen what has been done, or rather undone," cried the old priest with increasing emotion, "but surely you cannot expect me to approve the destruction of Catholic antiquity and symbolism, and the substitution of unmeaning and offensive novelties." "*Eh, patience*, Monsieur le curé; why I was going to propose to you to reform your church *à l'Italienne*, and to get rid of the monstrous barrack in the middle, *on les démonte partout*." At these words, the curé, reddening with indignation, exclaimed, "Monsieur de Chantal, the present degraded state of ecclesiastical discipline permits you, a layman in every respect but in the fashion of your clothes and the form of your peruke, to hold the highest office in a foundation where, in more ancient and better days, you would not have been permitted to take part in the most menial duties. You have destroyed that which your predecessors respected; you have defaced and mangled the Temple of God; you have dressed it out à la mode; and its solemnity is departed for ever, to the sorrow and disgust of myself and my people. But allow me to tell you, the parish church is under my care, and while I live not one stone of that venerable enclosure of the holy place shall be touched or removed, or its sacred imagery injured." The abbé, deeply mortified at the reproaches of the curé, endeavoured to conceal his mortification by diverting the discourse on the times and his parishioners. The curé, however, turning to his visitor, said in a sad and solemn tone, "The times are full of sad presage. The riches, the corruptions, immunities, and extravagant privileges that disgrace even the highest ecclesiastics of the land, are the subject of deep and merited murmurs among the neglected people; men begin to hate religion for the vices of its ministers, and those who squander in worldly vanity the revenues intended for the service of religion and Christ's poor, will have to give a fearful reckoning." The abbé started to his feet: "Nay, hear me," continued the curé. "You are one of these spoilers; it is true the abbey was given to you as a heritage, but it was the gift of those who had no power to bestow. Think of that choir, once filled with a hundred devout servants of God chanting his praises by night and day, now debased and almost deserted. The vast refectory in ruins,—its vaulted gateway, where hundreds partook the hospitality and charity of the house, now scarcely shelters a single straying mendicant—all is neglect and decay, and how will it end?" "Ah, mon Dieu," cried the abbé, "I cannot bear this; how often have I thought and tried for better things! But no, impossible. My rank, my family honour, all must be supported." So, hastily departing, he summoned his servants and carriage.—"To Paris!" he exclaimed. That night the Hotel de Chantal was a blaze of light, the rendezvous of the *élite* of the capital; and among the many cavaliers who escorted the fair dames of Paris that graced the mirrored and lustred saloons, none could surpass the gallantry and devotion of the noble owner of the mansion, the commendatory abbot of Conques....

Fifteen years had elapsed since that night of revelry—the Hotel de Chantal is closed—it has been pillaged of its costly furniture—its saloons are desolate: some few miserable people live in its upper rooms—a ferocious *sans-culotte* has replaced the liveried porter. Where is its once noble, its wealthy owner? In the corner of a miserable mansard of the Faubourg S. Germain crouched the figure of a man approaching the middle age, but whose unshaven visage and neglected state added several years to his appearance. His dress was that of a labourer, but the coarseness of his outer garments but ill accorded with his fair and unworked hands. A small leathern valise was by his side, and he anxiously listened to every sound. "This was the time he should have arrived," he exclaimed, "my retreat is only known to him. Mon Dieu! can he have betrayed me?" At this moment a confused and increasing sound of cries and snatches of songs was heard in the street—it is on the staircase—the tramp of ascending footsteps, mingled with imprecations of vengeance, strikes on the terrified ears of the unhappy Chantal, for such was the seeming labourer. He rushed to the window, but it afforded no chance of escape, as the eaves of the tiles were overhanging the street at a prodigious height, and the steepness of the pitch precluded all hope of ascending to the top. At this moment the door was assailed, the feeble fastenings soon gave way, and a party of men rushed in, among whom De Chantal distinguished his treacherous servant, who had betrayed his retreat. "Le voila!" he exclaimed, and in a moment the abbé was in the grasp of men who never spared an aristocrat. At the same time a red handkerchief held out of the window, announced to the crowd below that the victim had been captured and was secured, amid yells of triumph and execration. A few moments served to drag down the unfortunate abbé to the street, half filled by a mixed rabble, in which the women were conspicuous for their savage exclamations and menaces. "A bas les aristocrats, à bas les prêtres, à bas les tyrans," were heard on all sides, while the terrified abbé was forced along, strongly grasped by two ferocious *sans-culottes*.

In a short time they arrived at a small open space; some straw was scattered on the pavement, and by the side of a common butcher's block, hastily brought to the spot, stood a man of enormous muscular strength and lofty stature, a shirt loosely bound round his waist and a pair of sabots completed his attire, while he wielded a huge chopper or axe, in savage impatience for his victim. The abbé cast a terrified look at this popular executioner, and seemed indistinctly to recollect his ferocious features. "Oh, Jesu, Jesu," he shrieked, in agony of soul, when the furious infidel, bending towards him, in a voice of savage irony exclaimed, "*Il n'y est plus*, Monsieur l'Abbe; *nous l'avons démonté à Conques*, ha! ha!"—The executioner and the youth who cut away the rood were the same.—In a few moments a badly severed head and a bleeding corpse were tossed to and fro amid the frantic mob, and exposed to every indignity, till a common cart removed them and bore them to an unhallowed grave, and no cross ever marked the spot which held the mutilated remains of the last commendatory abbot of Conques, the *Pagan ambonoclast.*

THE REVOLUTIONARY AMBONOCLAST.

Jacques Frénin was the name of the man who so fearfully figured as the executioner of the abbé. From an early age he had imbibed those infidel opinions that were too industriously propagated among the French people for a considerable time previous to the breaking out of the great revolution. He hated the priests, because he thought they were rich, and not obliged to labour like himself; for the same reason he detested the nobility and higher classes. He considered religion as a mere invention of priestcraft; he was never seen at its offices, or participating in its rites; it was therefore not surprising that he assisted at the demolition of the ancient rood of the abbey with a sort of diabolical satisfaction. "Ma foi," he exclaimed, "c'était un beau commencement, mais ça ne s'arrêtera pas là;" and indeed, a few years later the full principles of infidelity developed themselves in the closing of all the temples of God, and total destruction of many of the most glorious religious monuments. As soon as popular fury had made head against all regular government, Jacques entered the National Guard, and proceeded to Paris, where his great strength and daring courage soon raised him in the estimation of his fiend-like associates. He was always the ready destroyer of a cleric or aristocrat; hence the terrible part he performed at the close of the last chapter. Through the continual occasions of plunder that presented themselves in those lawless times, he obtained a considerable sum of money, and with this he determined on retiring to his village, and securing some property. The abbey buildings had been nearly demolished for the materials, with the exception of the great western towers, which had resisted destruction, and stood now isolated, and of immense apparent height. Fragments of shafts, mullions, ribs, and ashlar-work were piled in heaps for sale, and the area of the church was one great mound of lime and broken materials. The sad scene of desolation produced no regret on the mind of the hardened Jacques, who merely exclaimed, "Ah, c'est fini!" and turned towards the old parish church, which was still standing. On drawing near he perceived an affiche announcing it for sale as part of the propriétés nationales. "Here is a capital chance," he thought; "a store for wood is what I require, and then if I buy that neighbouring forest my fortune is made." In a short time the purchase was concluded, and the venerable temple, which had for some time ceased to echo the divine praises, was disposed of to become a common wood-store. The interior of the building had a most desolate appearance; the whole was denuded of every ornament; the side altars were standing, but the high altar had been thrown down in a fruitless search for supposed treasure. An ancient image of our Lady had been removed, but the corbel remained, and the outline of the figure itself was traceable on the wall. The floor was strewed with rubbish, and damp was gathering round the bases of the pillars and chancel steps.

Jacques viewed his purchase with great satisfaction. Could he but fill it with wood, what profit he should realize! "But, peste!" he exclaimed, "with that diable de jubé, it is impossible to get a cart up near the end. Tu descendras vite." Now Frénin had assisted during his revolutionary campaigns at the destruction of many a noble church, and had remarked the expeditious way in which this was effected by cutting away the bases of the shafts, and propping them up with pieces of timber, smeared with pitch, which, when fired, were rapidly consumed, and caused the instant fall of the superincumbent weight; so that, as one of the writers of that period triumphantly explains, *"On peut détruire toute une cathédrale dans un petit quart d'heure."* Having frequently witnessed the success of this plan on a great scale, Jacques determined to apply it to the pillars of the rood screen, and with the aid of a mason who had been employed in the demolition of the abbey, he succeeded in stilting all the shafts on wooden shores, which he afterwards covered with grease and pitch. He calculated that in their fall they would bring in the vaulting of the loft, and, in fine, save all the trouble of pulling down piecemeal. All being prepared, he entered the church early in the morning, and twisting the wooden props with straw, he proceeded to ignite them. Those who have read the last chapter should remember the peculiar construction of this screen, with its iron trellis-work between the walls, the solid reredoses towards the chancel. A volume of smoke rose from each of the four piles of wood, succeeded by fierce crackling flames, and still denser smoke. Frénin was quickly escaping, when in the confusion of the moment, he pressed the iron gate from him; it closed with a spring catch, and with the rebound shot the key far beyond his reach into the nave. He rushed to the chancel doors, but they were barred within. In the midst of the increasing flame he frantically dashed himself now against the door, and now straining at the iron trellis, he roared with despair and terror; for at that early hour no one would be near to force the gates and save him. But two little children, belonging to a devout widow of the village, had been taught to go and offer their morning prayers before the church doors, though its portals had been closed for the ingress of the faithful; and, as usual, they bent their knees before the sacred threshold. Scarcely had they commenced their orisons, when the crackling sounds within the building attracted their attention; these were rapidly succeeded by the shouts of Frénin. Looking through the crevice, they beheld flames, and ran back affrighted to the village, exclaiming, "Le feu est à l'église." At this cry the peasants rushed from the houses, and the smoke, which now escaped from the broken windows of the edifice, showed that the alarm was too well founded. Proceeding to the western doors, which Frénin had closed on entering, they forced them open by means of a felled tree, swung by their united efforts as a ram.

On entering, the most horrible spectacle presented itself. The pillars and arches of the rood screen encircled in fire, and in the midst of smoke and blaze the gigantic figure of a man whose hair and clothes were already burning, yelling imprecations; in the agony of despair he grasped the bars with fruitless efforts to tear them from their faithful rivets. "Ah, mon Dieu, c'est Frénin," exclaimed the terrified villagers. "Il est perdu!" cried another voice, and at that instant the wooden shores, reduced to gleaming embers, gave way, and arches, vaulting, all fell in crushing weight on the wretched ambonoclast, who was speedily consumed beneath the burning mass. Water was now procured, and by the ready help of the numerous villagers who had been gathered to the spot, all danger to the fabric itself was soon prevented; but when the smoking ruins had been cleared away, a few ashes were all that remained of the powerful frame of Jacques Frénin, the revolutionary ambonoclast.

At this moment a man of venerable aspect entered the building, and who, notwithstanding his secular apparel, might still be recognized as the old curé, the Père Duchesne; for it was him, indeed. He had been concealed during the Reign of Terror by a neighbouring farmer, in whose loft the holy rites had often been privately celebrated. "My children," he exclaimed, "you behold the terrible judgments of God on those who sacrilegiously deface his holy temples. The unhappy Abbé de Chantal perished by the hand of that wretched man of whose awful death you have but just been the terrified spectators." A cry of subdued horror was heard among the listening people. "Yes," he continued, "I was an unwilling witness of his murder at Paris, and it was Frénin who struck the blow. Inured to every crime, a despiser of God's ordinances and of his ministers, he came at last to pollute this very temple to profane uses. But divine justice would not suffer this enormity; he has perished by his own hands, and his end was destruction. My dear children," continued the curé, "my heart bleeds to enter this church where I for so many years united with you in daily sacrifice and prayer, and from which we have been so long excluded, to see it so forlorn and desolate; and even now who knows but by my presence here I may be discovered and destroyed?" "Ah, mon père, mon père," murmured the villagers, "we will protect you." "God's will be done!" replied the curé. At that moment the sound of an approaching horseman was heard. The women instantly drew near the pastor, while some of the men hastened to the doors, to ascertain the person who was arriving. In a few moments they returned with a substantial farmer of the neighbourhood, covered with dust, who, hastening to the curé, exclaimed, "Ah, Monsieur le curé, nous sommes sauvés; le premier consul a restauré le culte," and handed a paper to the venerable priest, who could scarcely peruse it from emotion. It was, indeed, true; the concordat with the Holy Father was made, religion was restored. Such was the exultation of the inhabitants, that they would have had mass celebrated in the church, if the curé had not explained to them that, after its recent desecration, and the horrible death of Frénin, it would require reconciliation before any sacred rites could be performed within its walls; and for that purpose they must wait either for the bishop or his authority.

A procession in thanksgiving was then speedily arranged; and now with what alacrity long-concealed objects appeared! One good woman triumphantly produces a cope she had concealed under a quadruple layer of mattresses; another hastens with the holy water vat, brightening it up as she came along; half the contents of the ancient sacristy returned to view as if by magic. But what gave greater joy to the old curé than all the rest, was the ancient rood, that had been removed from the jubé and concealed in a roof by a pious parishioner. It came supported by four of the strongest youths, carried in triumph. The voice of the curé, enfeebled by age, and tremulous with overflowing devotion, could scarcely entone the Vexilla Regis, but it was instantly taken up by a chorus of voices. With caps in hand, tearful eyes, and swelling hearts, the villagers of Conques followed the venerable image of the Redeemer till arrived at the cemetery. The curé, after an ardent address of exhortation and thanksgiving, dismissed them with his blessing. One bell yet remained in the old tower; a rope was soon obtained, and loudly it rang on that happy day. The church was soon after reconciled, and the holy sacrifice has been continually offered up ever since. The rood was raised again on high, with great rejoicings, and Père Duchesne saw that day, and sang his *Nunc Dimittis*. He reposes in peace in the adjoining cemetery, but his spirit lives in his successor, who equally venerates the ancient traditions of his ancient faith. The rood is now safe from further profanation. The traces of Frénin's destruction will be shortly effaced by a perfect restoration; but the frightful end of the ambonoclasts of Conques will long form the subject of discourse among the inhabitants of the village.

THE MODERN AMBONOCLAST.

This character is of comparatively recent creation,—none of the species having been seen about in this country previous to the consecration of S. George's church. About that time two or three made their appearance, and, though not by any means in a flourishing condition, they have somewhat increased. It has been asserted that their first dislike of screens arose from a desire of literary notoriety, and that, finding several old women of both sexes had taken a most unaccountable and inexplicable offence at the ancient division of the chancel, and the restoration of the crucifix, which had been so wisely destroyed in the good old days of Queen Bess, they profited by the occasion to increase the sale of a periodical. But this may be mere calumny; and, indeed, it is very probable that it is a case of pure development, as at first they did not exhibit any repugnance to pointed churches, which they rather lauded, and only took objection to certain upright mullions and painful images; but they speedily developed other propensities and ideas, and latterly have exhibited symptoms almost similar to hydrophobia at the sight, or even mention, of pointed arches or pillars. The principal characteristics of modern ambonoclasts may be summed up as follows:—Great irritability at vertical lines, muntans of screens, or transverse beams and crosses; a perpetual habit of abusing the finest works of Catholic antiquity and art, and exulting in the admiration of everything debased, and modern, and trumpery; an inordinate propensity for candles and candlesticks, which they arrange in every possible variety; they require great excitement in the way of lively, jocular, and amatory tunes at divine service, and exhibit painful distress at the sound of solemn chanting or plain song; at divine worship they require to sit facing the altar, and near the pulpit, and then, if the edifice be somewhat like a fish-market, with a hot-water pipe at their feet, a gas-pipe in the vicinity, and a stove in the rear, they can realize a somewhat Italian atmosphere in cold and cheerless England, and revive some sparks of that devotion that the gloomy vaulting of Westminster and the odious pillars of a new rood screen had well nigh deprived them of. It must be, however, stated, to their credit, that the modern ambonoclasts, unlike their predecessors, confine their attacks to strokes of the pen; and we do not believe that they have hitherto succeeded in causing the demolition of a single screen. Indeed, it is probable that, if the development of their real character had not proceeded so rapidly, they might have caused some serious mischief to Catholic restoration; but the *cloven foot* is now so visible, that men are looking out in expectation of the *tail*, and are already on their guard.

CONCLUSION.

It now only remains to make some remarks on the recent revival of Catholic art and architecture, the difficulties with which it has to contend in England, and the opposition that has been raised against it. As the enclosures of the sanctuary can be traced from the erection of the earliest Christian churches, and as they are inseparably connected with reverence and solemnity, we might have hoped, and indeed expected, that the restoration would have been hailed by all who profess the ancient religion as an evidence of returning faith. But, alas, we have a class of men to oppose the revival of ancient symbolism, on whom the examples of fifteen centuries of Catholic antiquity fail to produce the slightest recognition of respect. The past is to them a nullity, and they would fain have us believe that the present debased externals of religion are to be equally received and propagated as those which were generated during the finest ages of Christian art. Now, knowing the whole history of this debasement in religious art, its origin and progress, and the general decline of Catholic faith and Catholic principles, corresponding to its increasing influence, it is impossible for us to regard its very existence otherwise than as an intolerable evil, and we must labour incessantly for its utter expulsion from our churches. The decline of true Christian art and architecture may be dated from a most corrupt era in the history of the church; and ever since that most unnatural adoption of Pagan externals for Catholic rites, we mourn the loss of those reverend and solemn structures which so perfectly embodied the faith for which they were raised. Bad as was the Paganism of the fifteenth and sixteenth centuries, it was dressed out in much external majesty and richness; but now nothing is left but the fag end of this system; bronze and marble are replaced by calico and trimmings; the works of the sculptor and the goldsmith are succeeded by the milliner and the toyshop; and the rottenness of the Pagan movement is thinly concealed by gilt paper and ribands,—the nineteenth century apeings of the dazzling innovations of the Medician era. Cheap magnificence, meretricious show, is the order of the day; something pretty, something novel, calico hangings, sparkling lustres, paper pots, wax dolls, flounces and furbelows, glass cases, ribands, and lace, are the ornaments and materials usually employed to decorate, or rather disfigure, the altar of sacrifice and the holy place. It is impossible for church furniture and decoration to attain a lower depth of degradation, and it is one of the greatest impediments to the revival of Catholic truth. It is scarcely possible for men to realize the awful doctrines and the majestic ritual of the Church under such a form; and yet these wretched novelties are found on the altars of some of the most venerable temples, equally as in the abortions of modern erection. They disfigure alike the cathedral of the city and the wayside chapel of the mountain-pass; they flourish in religious communities, and are even tolerated in the seminaries for the education of the priests of the sanctuary. Bad, paltry, miserable taste has overrun the externals of religion like a plague; and to this state of deplorable degradation would these new men bind our desires and intellects, as if it were of God, and on a par with the noble works achieved in times of zeal and faith, and at a period when all the art and talent of Christendom was devoted to the one object of increasing the glory and magnificence of the great edifices devoted to the worship of Almighty God. Moreover, it is very important to observe the extraordinary similarity of idea that actuated the artists of all Christian countries during the middle ages. Making due allowance for climate and materials, the same ruling spirit presided over the arts of Italy and England. The same devout effigies, recumbent and praying, each robed in the flowing ecclesiastical habits of the order, may be seen in every old Italian church, as in our own cathedrals. There was no difference then between a Roman chasuble and an English chasuble, between a Roman mitre and an English mitre. The same beautiful forms and proportions reigned universal. Even where the Christians extended their conquests in the East, in the city of Jerusalem itself, the edifices they raised were in architecture Pointed and Christian; some of which even still remain. Everywhere the Catholic might be traced by the works he raised; but now, alas, excepting by the extreme ugliness, and deformity, and paltry ornament, that are the usual characteristics of modern Catholic erections, it would be difficult to distinguish them from the recent productions of modern sects. Is it not a consideration that should fill every true Catholic heart with grief, that the propagation of the faith is no longer attended by the propagation of ecclesiastical traditions? Every year what zealous missionaries depart for distant climes, bearing with them, indeed, the true principles of faith, but with it the most degraded externals possible. The sources from whence they supply themselves are the magazines of Lyons and Paris, places filled with objects made entirely on the principle of cheap magnificence, uncanonical in form and often in material, hideous in design, utter departures from the beautiful models of mediæval antiquity, calculated only to please the vulgar and the ignorant, dazzling in the eyes of savages, but revolting to every man of true ecclesiastical knowledge and feeling. These things are not only expedited to the colonies and even to the antipodes to form in any mission a fresh nucleus of deplorable taste and ideas, but they inundate the sister island itself; yes, in Ireland, where, even in times considered barbarous, the ancient goldsmiths wrought exquisitely cunning work for the altar and the shrine, they now deck out her sanctuaries in Parisian trumpery, and borrow the model of her churches from the preaching-house of the Presbyterian settler; and to such a low ebb is all feeling for ecclesiastical art and architecture fallen—that when a cathedral is raised after the old form of the cross of Christ, its very bishop walls off the holy place, and converts it into *a room*! Room-worship, where all see, is the modern shell in which innovators and nineteenth-century men could *exhibit* those sacred mysteries for which Catholic antiquity raised those glorious choirs and chancels, witnesses of their reverence and our degeneracy. But sad to relate, this principle of room-worship is gradually extending itself into those majestic edifices of antiquity by the manner in which they are perverted to the modern system. The month of May is more especially devoted to the honour of our Blessed Lady, an excellent devotion, but how is it carried out? All who have had the misfortune of travelling on the continent during this month must have noticed an unusual disfigurement of the fabric in the shape of enormous festoons of red calico or some other material, as the case may be, pendent from the groining over a catafalque of painted canvass, flower-pots, and glass cases, surmounted by an image intended for our Blessed Lady herself, in the most meretricious attire covered with gauze and spangles. This miserable representation is usually set up in the very centre of the transept or the last bay of the nave, completely altering the whole disposition of a church. Great devotion to the blessed mother of our Lord, was a striking feature in mediæval antiquity. Almost every cathedral was dedicated in honour of Notre Dame, and where was the parish church of any size that did not possess its Lady chapel set apart for her peculiar honour? What beautiful examples have we of these in England, though, grievous to relate, some of them are converted to unworthy purposes, and all disused; but in many of the continental churches it is little better; for, except an occasional mass, Lady chapels, *as such*, are no longer kept up. In one of the finest churches of Liege I saw an altar set up for the month of May, a heap of paltry showy materials; but on getting to the other side I discovered this gilded front to be sustained by old packing-cases, trestles, casks, and planks, hastily piled up, and not even concealed from those who might penetrate eastward of the nave. Further on was the real Lady chapel in a very neglected state, without furniture or decoration: this was undoubtedly the portion of the church where the devotions of May should be celebrated; but the nave is more like a *room*, and is therefore used in preference to that portion of the fabric which the devout builders had set apart for the purpose. And what majestic Lady chapels did the old churches contain! usually the most eastward portion of the church,—the *refugium peccatorum*; they displayed in their windows and their sculptures all those edifying—those touching mysteries of our Lady's history which are so fruitful for contemplation, and the tryptych altar unfolded its gilded doors when adorned for sacrifice, with many a saint and angel depicted on its painted panels, and the office was sung by our Lady's chaplains, all in their stalls of quire, and the morrow mass-priest celebrated most solemnly, and many a taper burnt brightly before her image, and our Lady's chapel was one of the fairest portions of these fair churches. But now, alas, while these chapels are in a great measure abandoned to neglect, a wretched piece of scenery is substituted, and this is set up in the centre of the nave, to the disguise of the architecture and the impediment of its proper use. Even making all allowances for the reduced revenues of the continental churches, it must be admitted that they are for the most part most miserably neglected, and in a great measure disused. There are splendid crypts where no rites are ever celebrated. Lateral chapels turned into confessionals, or what is much worse, into deposits for lumber; everything is carried on on the smallest scale, and with the least trouble, and not only are the generality of modern Catholic churches on the continent most miserable abortions, but every year sad mutilations are permitted in many of those sacred buildings that are still preserved for religious purposes.

Even in the Pontifical States, within a very short period, a fine church, of mediæval construction, was shorn of both its aisles, by the act of the very canons themselves; one they demolished for the materials, and the other they converted into a custom house and stores. Indeed, many modern canons have been miserable stewards of the churches committed to their care, which makes their partial suppression in the eighteenth century the less to be regretted. As shown in the course of this work, they were great destroyers of choral arrangements and painted glass in the latter times; and from a much earlier period they were accustomed to raise a revenue by permitting domestic erections against the sacred edifices themselves, — shops and houses between buttresses and lodgments in porches.

At the north portal of Rouen cathedral but a few years since, I was obliged to climb into the roof of a wretched barrack or book-stall, erected in the seventeenth century, to inspect the unrivalled sculpture representing the creation of the world and the early Scripture history, and the very purloins of the roof were held by mortices cut into images of splendid design, and the rough walls built rudely against the most elaborate tabernacle-work and bas-reliefs. The tenants of these miserable shops, which gave the name of the Cour des Libraires to the northern approach of the cathedral, paid regular rent to the chapter down to the great revolution. I am happy to state that these unsightly excrescences have been demolished by the government, and the whole beauty of the original design is now visible.

At Aix-la-Chapelle, a city reported, and, I believe, with truth, to be full of devout persons, the Dom is incumbered with houses and shops for the sale of snuff-boxes, pipes, and tobacco, between every buttress of the apsis surrounding the high altar, and the owners of these habitations are driving their bargains and cooking their victuals within a few feet of the high altar of a church which is the depository of the most venerable reliques of Europe. I mention these things to show how sadly the ancient reverence of sacred buildings and things has declined in latter times, and most assuredly they are intimately connected with the screen question. Rites so sacred as those of the Catholic church require every watchfulness, both in conduct and in externals, to preserve them in due veneration; and an irreverent arrangement in the construction of a church may be the cause of infinite sin and scandal. Now, therefore, that we are beginning, as it were, *de novo*, to restore the churches of God, how important is it that we should so construct them, that they may by their symbolic and ancient fashion, set forth the stupendous mysteries for whose celebration they are raised, and, at the same time, prove them to belong to that very faith that generated, centuries ago, those great principles of Christian art which we may rival, but scarcely excel!

The Catholic body in England is now suddenly become the spectacle of the world. An immense responsibility has been incurred; how will it be supported? Our episcopal rulers bear titles which are associated with the most venerable men and places in the history of the English church, — names associated with the first planting of Christianity in this land, — names known far and wide as pertaining to some of the fairest fabrics that Catholic hands ever raised to the honour of their Creator, — and names the very possession of which in a manner demand a conduct and principles in accordance with their import. May we not then hope, nay, expect, that better times are approaching; that our spiritual rulers will, in very deed, set forth, if not the full glories of the ancient men, at least a continuation of their principles, so that, in all the works undertaken under their auspices, the old spirit and intention may be evident. Christian architecture must now become a *principle*, and not a *mere matter of whim and caprice of individuals*, or its advocacy or rejection treated as a mere jest. Architects may suggest and execute, *but the moving power must come from episcopal authority—that is the legitimate source*. The finest churches, unless the ecclesiastics enter into the spirit of the arrangement and construction, are only so many evidences of modern degeneracy; and the erection of a choral church for an orchestral service is a farce, and a prostitution of ancient symbolism to a profane and irreverent purpose, even more painful than when it is carried on in a meeting-house with an altar in it. And as for those men who would import the debased modern externals of Italy into this land for religious purposes, whatever their intentions may be, *they can only be practically considered as the greatest and worst enemies with which we have to contend*, for they lower the majesty of religion to the level of a common show, and degrade the sacrament before the people, giving occasion for scoffing and ridicule, and putting stumbling-blocks in the way of our separated countrymen, dressing up the altar of God like a mountebank's show, and imparting a strange and modern appearance to that which was indeed the ancient faith of this land. What a mockery would it be to lead those devout men, (who though separated in position, have been united in heart with the ancient religion, who have prayed in deserted aisles and chapels, kissed the prostrate consecrated stones of ancient sacrifice, and mourned over desecrated shrines and rifled tombs of holy dead,) up to the threshold of that very gate within which they fondly hoped for the realization of all those glories on which they have existed for years, on its being opened, to introduce them into a sort of drawing-room chapel with a deal altar hung with gauze, lace, and ribands, surmounted by a *chiaro oscuro* of an ecstatic friar dancing a naked Bambino in his arms, and a bason on a neat stool for a font. "Impostors," they would exclaim, "is this the realization of the ancient faith? why, the wreck we have left savours more of the old spirit than this miserable show." But let us reverse the scene, and introduce our pilgrims into a church, raised after the ancient fashion of those in which they had been used to worship, but restored to life and beauty. First, that veiled altar and ardent lamps tell of the divine presence abiding among men: *ecce tabernaculum Dei cum hominibus*. What sanctity this imparts to the whole fabric, and how dead do even the most stupendous churches appear when denuded of the sacramental presence; the ground itself in such a place is holy: not only the disposition of the fabrick itself, but every enrichment, every detail harmonises in setting forth one grand illustration of the faith. The windows sparkle in saintly imagery and sacred mysteries, the very light of heaven enters through a medium which diffuses it in soft and mellowed hues. What a perspective is presented to the sight, of successive pillars supporting intersecting arches, leaving distant openings into aisles and chapels! Then the chancel, with its stalled quire seen through the traceried panels of the sculptured screen, above which, in solemn majesty, rises the great event of our redemption, treated after a glorified and mystical manner, the ignominious cross of punishment changed into the budding tree of life, while, from the tesselated pavement to the sculptured roof, every detail sets forth some beautiful and symbolical design; how would such a fabric strike to the heart of a devout soul, seeking for the realization of ancient solemnities! And is it not a case of gross infatuation for men professing the old faith to reject what we may truly imagine to be a revelation made by the mercy of God for the consolation of his servants upon earth, and to turn back to the old vomit of Pagan design, associated only with the infernal orgies of false gods and heathen corruptions? Does it not show an utter loss of all appreciation of the beautiful and the true, and a state of mental degradation as deplorable, as it is alarming in its practical results?

Yes, it is mainly to these causes that the reproaches of debasement, that are so frequently urged against us by Protestants, are to be traced, nor can we scarcely wonder that those who judge by externals and do not penetrate beneath the surface, should come to such conclusions, judging by what is presented before them even under the most glorious vaults of Christendom. But when we turn to true Catholic art, what do we behold? the works of men profoundly versed in symbolism and the holy scriptures: indeed, the great portals of the foreign cathedrals are *Bibles in stone*. There we trace the sacred history from the first moving of the spirit of God on the waters to the creation of all matter and man himself; there we are led down through the Mosaic history to the prophets foretelling the redemption of man, each with his phylactery and appropriate emblem; beside those, all the types of the old law, those mystical foreshadowings of our blessed Lord and his passion, till we come to the realities, and every scene and every mystery connected with the redemption of man, from the angelical salutation to the ascension into heaven, are so severely, yet so piously treated, that they at once address themselves to the inquiring mind of childhood, and draw tears of devout admiration from mature and reflective age. O, spirit of ancient Catholic art, how is it that you no longer abide among its people? What curse, what blight, has deprived us of your aid? Is it not that the sons of the church have forsaken the old traditions of faith, and have gone straying after strange forms and gods, and substituted debased novelties for ancient excellence, and to these profane and irreverent representations they have given the name of Christian saints, using the mysteries of religion as a mere peg whereon to hang their abominable productions.

This system prevailed to such an extent that, in the sixteenth and seventeenth centuries, the people, and even the historians themselves, lost all knowledge of what some of the sculptures of their very cathedrals represented, and explained the prophecies of scripture and the histories of the Old Testament by modern legends,[21] with which they were not in the least connected, as may be seen in the histories of Amiens, Rouen, &c.

There can be no doubt that in modern art the great and important mysteries of Catholic truth have been in a great manner supplanted by the representations of novel devotions and dubious representations.[22] Among these latter, heart paint-

---

[21] In the old histories of Amiens, the bas-relief representing the prophecy of Micheas, cap. iv., v. 3, "Et concidant gladios suos in vomeres, et hastas in ligones," was commonly described as representing the ancient manufacture of arms, for which that city was celebrated, but to which it has not the slightest reference. At Rouen, the history of Joseph and his brethren, with their sacks, and the cup, with the hanging of the chief butler, was considered as that of a cheating corn-factor, by the seizure of whose property the portal was erected; but without the smallest grounds of probability, as shown by the learned Dom Pomeraye.

[22] It is worthy of remark that the idea of representing S. Joseph holding our Lord in

ing has a most extraordinary vogue. Without being wanting in the respect due to the authorized devotion of the sacred heart, I should be deficient in duty as a Christian artist if I did not protest most strongly and candidly against the external form in which it is usually represented. It is quite possible to embody the pure idea of the divine heart under a mystical form that should illustrate the intention without offending the sense; but when this *most spiritual idea* is depicted by an anatomical painting of a heart copied from an original plucked from the reeking carcase of a bullock, and done with sickening accuracy of fat and veins, relieved on a chrome yellow ground, it becomes a fitting subject of fierce denunciation for every true Christian artist, as a disgusting and unworthy representation for any object of devotion. The rage that appears to exist among many modern communities for hearts, is quite astonishing. To a casual observer of some of their oratories it would really appear that their whole devotion consisted in this representation: it is depicted in every possible form and variety, sometimes *revolvant* and smoking, sometimes *volant*, with a pair of wings growing out of the sides, sometimes *ardent*, flaming, fizzing, bursting like an exploding shell, sometimes *nayant*, floating in a pool, sometimes in pairs, sometimes in clusters. In fine, we have them in every possible variety, and they are by no means dissimilar to the illustrations of those amatory epistles so largely circulated in this country about the feast of S. Valentine. Whether there lingers any association of ideas between these latter and their more spiritual counterparts in the minds of pious ladies, I do not pretend to determine, but most certainly these vile caricatures have a wonderful hold of the fair sex, whose very book-marks generally consist of such representations. Moreover, the bad and vicious taste that prevails in the greater part of our religious communities of women, is a very serious evil;[23] many of them are houses of education, and it

---

his arms is comparatively modern, and in utter opposition to the ancient school of Christian art, who always ascribed a secondary position to this saint, and never made any representation of him that would convey the least idea of his entertaining any *paternal* affection for our Blessed Lord. I have attentively studied this subject, and never yet found any ancient representation that does not fully bear out my assertion. This is one of the many instances where modern art, disregarding ancient traditions, seeking the pretty and the pleasing, in lieu of the mysterious and sublime, has imparted the externals of importance to S. Joseph that the church has never recognized. *Our Divine Lord as an infant was always represented in the arms of the Blessed Virgin, and no other*, in all ancient mosaic painting and sculpture, and I believe that these modern images of S. Joseph, which have such astonishing vogue among devout people, if brought before an episcopal council, would be condemned as tending towards erroneous opinions.

[23] The usual description of articles made by nuns in their recreation were produced by scissors and paste, little gilt paper nick-nacks, fit only to please children of a very tender age, and, indeed, bad for them, as tending to corrupt their early notions. Every convent had a glass-case, in which their miserable productions were reserved, and shown and sold to visitors. I have heard of a very devout man, a member of the English church, who went to see a convent in the centre of England, imbued with the most reverent idea of conventual architecture; cloisters, chapter-houses, oratories, dim oriels, and all the associations of old religious buildings. What, therefore, was his astonishment, at being driven up to what he conceived, from its external appearance, was a new parochial union; nor was it lessened on his being shown into a modern-looking, ill-furnished parlour, containing one of these glass-cases full of trumpery, and invited to become a purchaser; when, in his confusion, he

is most lamentable that, with the first elements of religion and piety, the pupils imbibe the poison of bad and paltry taste which, from early associations, affects them perhaps through life, and vitiates all their ideas on those subjects connected with the externals of religion. It is true that, by the blessing of God, the principles of Catholic art are by degrees penetrating these strongholds of prejudice and bad taste, but as yet I am not aware of one house of education where there is even a decent chapel; the great reforms have been effected among the active orders of ladies, and I will most fearlessly appeal to their convents, where trash of every kind has been excluded, where both the needle and pen reproduce the beautiful ornaments of antiquity, and where the united voices of the community send forth the old Gregorian tones from their stalls, as examples of what may be done by those who, even with slender human means, apply themselves to the revival of true Catholic art and practices. But this is only in England, and I fear that, at the present time, nearly the whole conventual system on the continent is sunk in the production of the veriest trash that was ever contrived for the desecration of the altar and degradation of ecclesiastical costume. What an appalling field of labour lies before the missionaries of Christian art! Yet the very magnitude of the task should only serve to animate its disciples to heroic exertion in its propagation, and to rescue the Catholic faith from the external degradation into which it has fallen, and to reinstate it in all its former majesty, and to restore the reverend usages of the ancient fabrics, by which the sacred mysteries of the church may be set forth in a more lively and striking manner, strengthening the zeal and devotion of the faithful and drawing to the fountain of truth those souls whom the theatrical choirs and modern abuses have deterred from uniting.

If men were but acquainted with the Catholic church as she really is, in her canons, and her authoritative service books, how differently would they think and speak of her! The majesty of the language used in her ritual and pontifical is inferior only to that of the sacred scriptures themselves, and would almost seem to bear the evidence of inspiration in the text. How we must admire the appropriate fitness of each consecration to the peculiar object to be devoted to the service of Almighty God, from the walls of the temple and altar of sacrifice to those heralds of solemnity, the bells, whose brazen notes can animate a whole population with one intention and one prayer! Then if we consider the divine song of the church, its serenity, its melody, and indeed its almost sacramental power in infusing faith into the heart as its tones flow into the ears of the assistants, while the rhythm most perfectly expresses the sense of the sacred words thus solemnly sung, without vain repetitions and distracting fugues, but as is ordered by the Roman ceremoniale, sit devota, distincta, et intelligibilis, so that men listen, not to curious sounds, but sing in prayer and with one voice, glorify God in unison of heart and sound. found himself the fortunate possessor, minus seven shillings, of a paper donkey and two paniers of sugar-plums, and was glad to make a speedy retreat, with this singular reminiscence of the modern daughters of S. Benedict. It is, however, a great satisfaction to know that a better spirit is arising in several cloistered communities, who now reproduce the sacred vestments in the integrity of form; and we may hope and trust that the time is not far distant when all the external objects of these convents will harmonize with the venerable habit they wear, and with that internal spirit of piety which they have so wonderfully maintained amid degenerate taste.

What majestic, what consoling services has the church provided for her children! What happiness, even on earth, might they not realize by fulfilling the loving intentions of such a mother, and by devoting their means and energies, carry out the authorized and ancient ritual! But alas, such is the degenerate spirit of this age, that even among those who profess the ancient faith in this land, the existence of solemn services is the exception and not the rule; and while this is the case how can we wonder at the feelings with which they are regarded by the majority of our separated countrymen, who from curiosity or better motives of inquiry attend them? A great portion of the old country missions have usually a sort of room with a look of chilling neglect, at one end of which a wooden sarcophagus or quatrefoil box serves for an altar, duly supplied with some faded artificials and mean candlesticks of a culinary pattern. A mouldy picture of the bad Italian school, given by some neighbouring patron on account of its worthlessness to the chapel, hangs above. A cupboard, painted in marble streaks, serves for a tabernacle; a half-parlour, half-kitchen, for a sacristy and confessional, damp and neglected; and a range of benches, with kneeling boards, provided with every description of carpet patch and moth-eaten cushions, complete the fittings of these establishments; and here, Sunday after Sunday, is a short said mass, badly responded by some poor lad, a large amount of English prayers, with a discourse, &c. &c. This is the only service which the congregation hear on the greatest festivals; to them the solemn offices of Holy Week and the alleluias of the Paschal time are equally unknown. A poor priest, ill supported and alone, without means and persons to aid in his functions, abandons the glories of religion in despair, and thinks himself truly fortunate if he can secure the essential sacraments to those committed to his charge. But what is the consequence? Though the old people, from long habit, are content with this state of things, their children do not imbibe any of that zeal and Catholic spirit that the glorious offices of the church infuse into the tender mind, —that love of the house of God and of his service, —that interest which the succeeding and varied festivals awake in the youthful heart; and, sad to relate, many of the old congregations are decaying, and some have already *died out*. Now, if this state of things was the result of absolute unavoidable poverty, it would seem cruel to allude to it; but I grieve to say, many of these sort of places are sustained, or pretended to be sustained, by old and wealthy families, who, out of abundant fortunes, dole a much worse pittance to the chaplain than the butler: and who, to avoid the inconvenience of people coming too near their habitations, have fitted up an unoccupied stable, or an old outhouse, for the tabernacle of the living God!! This is no overdrawn picture, and I draw it to try if public shame can work on these men, who seem dead to every other. Why, there are estates possessed by nominal Catholics so broad, that six parochial churches might be raised, and filled with the faithful; and yet, perhaps in this vast space is only one wretched room like that described for all the Catholic community, thus depriving more than two-thirds of the Catholic population of even the practical means of fulfilling the duties of their religion! It is a common cry that the Catholic body are poor, —but it is false: the bishops are poor, the clergy are poor, the masses of town population are poor; but there is wealth yet in possession of men who have not altogether renounced the name, although they have the practice of Catholics (if the world and Satan did not grasp their hands), to restore religion throughout England, and to place it in such a position as to be a beacon and a light to all. What, then, must be the black despair of one of these men, when the world to whom he has sacrificed all is passing away from him for ever! His gay companions of the turf who have cheated him, and fattened on his rents and lands, have left him to die alone,—not one of these jovial friends are there. A few mercenary attendants hover round, to watch the last, and divide what they may. No chapel or chaplain: the priest has long been driven out to live on a distant portion of the property; the old chapel is a disused garret, where a few moth-eaten office-books and unstrung beads tell of the departed piety of the older members of the family. But many years have elapsed since holy rites or holy men were there seen or heard. Stupified with disease, the wretched owner of a vast estate, childless and deserted, draws near his end. He has wasted a life which might have been one of usefulness and honour. He has impaired a property which was ample enough to have enabled him to have placed the religion of his fathers on a noble footing; he might have founded missions, established schools, encouraged his tenants, and been the means of bringing numerous souls to God. But he has done nothing—he has got nothing, but the whitening bones of some racers that cost him thousands, lost him thousands, and were shot in an adjoining paddock, and stocks of empty bottles, consumed in entertaining worthless associates, and a broken constitution now bearing him to a premature end. It is over. He is no more. Unrepentant, unshriven, unanealed, his spirit has gone to judgment. No ministers of God, no rites of holy church, were there to exhort and strengthen the departing soul. There was not one of all those mighty consolations which the church has provided for dying Christians and their survivors. No stoled priests kneel around in prayer and supplication; no ardent lights show forth the glorious hope of resurrection; no poor bedesmen receive the funeral dole, and cry, "May God have mercy on him!" no solemn knell invites the departing prayer; the chamber of death is close and still: the Protestant undertaker encloses the festering corpse in costly coffins, hideous in form and covered with plated devices, but not one Christian emblem among them all; a huge pile of sable feathers, as if in mockery, surmounts the whole; and thus it stands, till, in a few days, it is committed to moulder in the old vault. Placed on the north side of an old parish church that had been built for Catholic rites, but now blocked up with unsightly pews and galleries of uncouth and rude construction, and denuded of every ancient decoration, the family vault had once stood within a chantry, but the roof had long disappeared, while the walls were crumbled into shapeless mounds. In the midst of a small space, rank with weeds and nettles, was a huge brick tomb railed in with bar and spike. A slippery way dug out at the lower end showed a rapid descent to a dark aperture, formed by the removal of a large stone, piled against the side. Over this stood the clergyman of the parish, in a loosely fitting surplice ill concealing his semi-lay attire beneath, attended by a decrepit clerk, who alternately recited the appointed office. The executor, the lawyer, and the undertaker's men, with some curious lookers-on, are alone present at this sad and desolate spectacle. The coffin is lowered down the incline, the heavy mass is forced into its narrow space, jammed in amongst the mouldering shells of older interments. The men issue from the vault—the stone is replaced—the heavy fall of earth clods resound on its hollow surface, and as the access is filled in, all depart—the executors to the will—the undertakers to the nearest tavern. Two old men linger on the spot. "Well," one exclaimed, "I would not have thought the squire would have died thus." "Alack, alack!" replied his companion, "it was all along of bad company. I have heard Father Randall say, many a time, *he were a good young man.*" It was so indeed, *he was a good young man.* He was taught and fulfilled his duties, but he never knew the grandeur or the majesty of the faith in which he was reared. It was not his pride, his glory. He knew it only as the persecuted—the contemned religion of his ancestors, to which he was bound to adhere, but he never felt its power, nor understood it as the fountain, the source of all that is majestic, true, and ennobling upon earth, and so, when he heard it laughed at as an old-fashioned jest, and got entangled with worldly men, he abandoned its observances by degrees, and sunk into worldly pleasures and feelings till he became dead to every call of conscience, even for the most essential duties of religion, and came to that miserable end. If this illustration be considered unsuitable for an architectural work, I reply that the revival of true architecture is intimately mixed up with education and the formation of the minds of the rising Catholic generation. It is during the first few years of mental training that the character and feelings are generally formed, and I maintain the moral part of Catholic architecture, that is to say, the fitting of the mind to understand and appreciate the external beauties of religion, and to produce that love of God's service in the youthful heart, is quite as important, and can only be raised in places where the offices of religion are solemnly performed, and in suitable edifices. Now this should be most strictly considered for the education of both clergy and laity, for while the clergy have to officiate in these edifices, and carry out their various uses, it is to the laity that they must look both for the funds for the erection and the necessary means of support after they are erected. Therefore, it is of paramount importance that both receive the initiations in this matter, for early impressions are everything. How truly deplorable are the ordinary class of chapels attached to bishops' seminaries in France, for the most part whitewashed saloons, without anything ecclesiastical about them, except bad pictures, worse even than the walls they cover. Fortunately, they are usually in the vicinity of some fine old church, where the ecclesiastical students assist occasionally; but still, all should be in harmony, the seminary with the cathedral, and the clergy with both.

In respect of collegiate chapels we are certainly far in advance in England, but one great chapel, very nearly completed, yet lingers on in an unfinished state, when a little effort might render it available for divine service, and, in the meantime, many students must quit the college without that true love of ecclesiastical art that is only imparted to the soul by a devout assistance at the functions of religion in these solemn edifices. The mere inspection of them is nothing, it is when they become associated with the life of divine worship that they produce the full power and lift the soul in ecstasy. Let us hope and pray that not only in colleges, but in all places set apart for the education of youth, suitable chapels may be provided, so as to make the students love the beauty of God's house. I must confess, with every wish to preserve my charity, I am moved to indignation when I hear proposals for erecting great sheds to serve as Catholic churches, places resembling a depot for railway goods or the housings of a wharf. What treatment is this for the divine mysteries! what treatment for the poor, who are brought to worship God in a place little, if any, better than the union, or market shambles themselves! One of the many great benefits conferred by church architecture, is its affording the poor man a glorious edifice where he may enter at will; his position of course shuts him off from participating in all worldly grandeur or magnificence, but the portal of the Catholic church is open to him early and late; there he is no intruder, he may rest on the marble pavement or kiss the costliest shrine—he is spurned from every other ground and noble edifice but this—and yet this new system would bring the churches down to a level with the offices of a parish workhouse, and deprive him for ever of so great a consolation as the sight and enjoyment of a solemn pile. No blessing can be expected for those who erect the temples of God in a sparing and commercial calculating spirit. It is a positive insult to divine providence to build a church on such low and niggard principles, calculated to draw down a curse instead of a blessing. It is contrary to first principles: if we saw a man pretending to make an offering to us, in which he had economized in every possible manner, should we be disposed to receive his gift with the same feelings as for another who poured out his offering in a heartfelt and abundant manner? From those who have little it shall be taken away, and it is impossible to conceive any blessing attending one of these cast iron shells. It now remains briefly to consider the actual revival of Christian architecture among the English Catholic body, and to point out some important practical principles which are as yet but imperfectly understood.

In restoring the ecclesiastical architecture of the middle ages, there are certain modifications and changes which the altered position of religion renders absolutely necessary; for instance, in erecting a cathedral or bishop's church it should be so arranged as to *be perfectly available for the public worship of the faithful*, and the choir, on that account, should not be enclosed in a solid manner, but with open screens like the great parochial churches at Lubeck, and many other continental cities, and also not unfrequently in England, as at Newark, a grand parochial church; S. Nicholas, Lynn; Great Yarmouth, Southwold, and many other such edifices intended for parochial worship.

These churches may be as spacious and magnificent as cathedrals, as indeed many of them are, but perfectly adapted for a great body of people assisting at the sacred rites. It was currently reported that the learned Père Martin declared that the old screens contributed to the loss of faith among the people. Now if the reverend father did make this statement, I have no hesitation in contradicting it, and for this reason, that in those times when the cathedrals had enclosed choirs, they were erected and used for the purpose of keeping up a great choral service, and a worship of Almighty God *irrespective of popular assistance*; but coeval with these were multitudes of grand parochial churches like S. Maclou, at Rouen, relatively as magnificent as cathedrals, and where there never existed any enclosed choirs at all, but open ones, as I have shown in this work; it appears therefore that the assertion of the reverend father has been made hastily, and without sufficient grounds.

At the present time, when we are almost on the apostolic system of the primitive times, a cathedral should be perfectly adapted for parochial as well as episcopal use, which was indeed the ancient arrangement in corresponding times of antiquity when neither churches nor clergy were very numerous.

The next important point is the arrangement of the chancels, that they may be perfectly adapted for the easy access and egress of large bodies of communicants which have greatly increased since the middle ages. The chancels of all large town churches should be continued either like apsidal choirs, or taken out of the body of the church with the aisles continuing eastward on either side, and terminating in chapels, thus permitting the free egress of those who have communicated without returning through the holy doors. This arrangement is not of any importance in country parishes where the number of communicants is necessarily limited, and where the elongated chancels may be retained, but in great towns it is almost indispensable. And this leads us to another matter of considerable importance. Almost all the pointed churches that have been erected in towns, have been taken from examples in the country villages, and although low churches built of rubble walls with broach spires look most beautiful and appropriate amid cottages, elm trees, and rural scenery, they appear quite out of place when transplanted among the lofty mansions and scenery of a great city. A church has recently been erected in London the design of which *per se* is exceedingly pleasing, but instead of the sky line of the gable roofs we have the attic story and Roman cement balustrades and hideous chimney-pots of an adjoining terrace rising above them.

In all ancient cities where the houses were lofty, *the churches were the same*, as at Antwerp, Bruges, Ghent, Lubeck, Ratisbonne, Nuremberg. There are houses in the old towns whose gables are much higher than are our first-rate houses, but the churches rise very far above them, so that when seen from a considerable distance, the temples of God appear over all surrounding objects. Moreover, internal grandeur can only be produced by great height; it is a most important feature, and one which cannot be exaggerated, therefore I hope and trust that in future erections, no false economy, will interfere with this important and symbolic principle. Another point to be considered in the erection of town churches is the approach or entrance, which, if it be possible, should be contrived through a cloister or porch, answering to the ancient atrium. This would not only prevent noise and break currents of air, but it would serve to prepare the mind of the worshipper before entering the church itself, as a most devotional effect might be imparted to the cloister by sculptures and paintings, of which there are examples in several churches of Cologne and other cities in Germany. I believe these would be found most advantageous, not only for these religious reasons, but as completely shutting off the ingress of external cold air,[24] and the church itself might be free from drafts and

---

[24] The clumsy manner in which the old church-doors were fitted, and their opening direct into the body of the building, combined with the length of Protestant sermons, have been the primary cause of pews. In many churches they were almost necessary to protect the legs and head from cutting drafts; and if these pews are now removed, and replaced by open seats, without remedying the doors and currents of cold air, the old partitions will return. The first thing is to remove the cause—the effect will follow. Long sermons, also, have contributed much to pew-making. A person assisting at an office where there is frequent change of posture does not attach much importance to his seat, but when he is fixed for a whole hour's sitting, the case is different; and hence the comfortable contrivances in the modern English churches where the sermon is everything, and the divine offices and litur-

yet properly ventilated from above. And it is a great point for the revival of true church architecture, that it should be practically convenient both for clergy and people, and that it is quite possible to preserve an even temperature in the largest buildings is proved at S. Peter's, Rome, and which really constitutes its greatest—if not its only merit.

It is also most essential to erect spacious sanctuaries, and cloisters for the vesting of the singing clerks, who should not enter the priests' sacristy, and they should be so contrived as not to be converted to rooms of passage, or where women could find any excuse for penetrating. The sacristies of the old Italian churches are magnificent, both in dimensions and decorations. They are like second churches; and, indeed, they should be considered and treated with nearly equal respect on account of the sacred vessels and ornaments that are reserved within their ambries. But to erect these noble adjuncts to churches some considerable funds must be granted, and architects must not be expected, as has fallen to my lot, to build a sacristy and fittings for £40, and find some candlesticks into the bargain.

Our churches should now combine all the beauty and symbolism of antiquity with every convenience that modern discovery has suggested, or altered ecclesiastical discipline requires. The revival would then become a living monument and a true expression of the restoration of religion in the land. But I grieve to say, from what I see of the majority of pointed churches now erecting, that they are calculated to inflict greater injury on the cause than even the Italian abortions, which can only excite disgust, and drive men to the opposite opinion, and therefore practically of some service. It is now time that the movement assumed a regular principle; in the commencement everything was strange and ill understood; step by step we had to fathom, and works which now appear easy of execution were then deemed almost impracticable. A great many errors and failures were the natural consequence, and no man has been guilty of greater mistakes than myself; some of them were caused by want of experience in this new and difficult career, others through total inadequacy of funds. However, I feel certain that, but a few years ago, even unlimited funds could not have produced a truly fine work; and now I believe that a very majestic building could be accomplished at a comparatively moderate outlay. But I am sorry to say that, as yet, I see no man who has profited by my original errors. The new churches are more elaborate and full of decoration, but as convenient buildings are rather a decline from those originally produced, and much more costly and very unsuitable for their intentions. There is no distinction between churches intended for religious orders and those for parochial purposes, though their use is widely different. Formerly every order built in accordance with its own rules, and it is easy, on the mere inspection of these buildings, to ascertain their origin. The Dominicans were great preachers, and consequently their churches are like immense naves, with lateral chapels between the buttresses; the high altar placed against a reredos, behind which was the choir for the religious. Christian architecture lends itself perfectly to all these varieties: a Carthusian, a Dominican, or a Franciscan church may be and *were* quite in accordance with true ecclesiastical architecture, and yet most differently disposed, to suit the various religious rules.

gy but little considered. Pews are essentially Protestant, but I have seen incipient erections of the sort even in Catholic churches.

Unless Pointed architecture is carried out on these adaptive rules, which are the old ones, it is not a living monument. It is quite certain that our present race of architects, as a body, do not yet understand the language: they transcribe words, and even sentences, accurately, but it is a dead imitation of something already done, and not a living creation; and, consequently, great sums are thrown away in fine and praiseworthy and well-intentioned attempts, but which will be shortly deplored by all concerned. I grieve to see this, as, unless it is remedied, it may be the means of giving the Pagans a *temporary* triumph. I say temporary, because their eventual destruction is as certain as that of the power of the devil himself, but, like him, they have done and may do a deal of mischief till they are finally bound.

I therefore most earnestly conjure all those men who profess to revive true architecture to look to the wants and circumstances of the time, *not to sacrifice principles, but to prove that the real principles can combine with any legitimate requirement of religion*; let the bishops and clergy practically perceive that Christian architecture fulfils perfectly all their wants: let there be light, space, ventilation, good access, with the absence of drafts, which destroy devotion and excite prejudice against Pointed doorways. Avoid useless and over-busy detail, and rely on good proportions and solemnity of effect. Above all, we must remember that everything old is not an object of imitation—everything new is not to be rejected. If we work on these golden principles, the revival would be a living monument, as it was in days of old; and that God may grant us means to carry it out, that he will enlighten the hearts of the obdurate, and unite the faithful in one great bond of exertion for the revival of the long-lost glory of his church, sanctuary, and altar, is the earnest prayer of the writer of this book.

FINIS.

Lector House believes that a society develops through a two-fold approach of continuous learning and adaptation, which is derived from the study of classic literary works spread across the historic timeline of literature records. Therefore, we aim at reviving, repairing and redeveloping all those inaccessible or damaged but historically as well as culturally important literature across subjects so that the future generations may have an opportunity to study and learn from past works to embark upon a journey of creating a better future.

This book is a result of an effort made by Lector House towards making a contribution to the preservation and repair of original ancient works which might hold historical significance to the approach of continuous learning across subjects.

HAPPY READING & LEARNING!

LECTOR HOUSE LLP
E-MAIL: lectorpublishing@gmail.com

www.ingramcontent.com/pod-product-compliance
Lightning Source LLC
Chambersburg PA
CBHW020734160726
47993CB00006B/2443